To Peggy, and in men

WILLIAM SPEIRS BRUCE

POLAR EXPLORER AND
SCOTTISH NATIONALIST

PETER SPEAK

Peter Speak

[SPRI]

NATIONAL MUSEUMS OF SCOTLAND
PUBLISHING

Published by NMS Publishing
a division of NMS Enterprises Limited
National Museums of Scotland
Chambers Street
Edinburgh EH1 1JF

ISBN 1-901663-71-X

British Library Cataloguing in Publication Data
A catalogue record of this book
is available from the British Library.

Design by NMS Publishing, NMS Enterprises Limited.
Printed and bound in Great Britain by Bath Press Ltd, Bath.

CONTENTS

ACKNOWLEDGEMENTS

WILLIAM SPEIRS BRUCE was a great correspondent, sometimes writing twice in one day to the same person, or sending telegrams. In addition to the many documents held at the Scottish Oceanographical Laboratory, many papers were deposited with Bruce's lawyer, Alfred N Aitken. When Aitken died in 1947, a large chest of papers relating mostly to the Scottish National Antarctic Expedition was brought to the Scott Polar Research Institute in Cambridge by Sir James Mann Wordie. Further archive material is held in the University of Edinburgh, the National Museums of Scotland, and the libraries of the Royal Scottish Geographical Society and Royal Geographical Society in London.

This new biography of Bruce is based on research into the extensive archives of personal letters, scientific records, books, photographs and maps that survive in Cambridge, Edinburgh, Glasgow and London. It has been published as a tribute to Bruce – 'the Forgotten Polar Hero' – to commemorate the centenary anniversary in 2002 of the departure of *Scotia* for Antarctica. Acknowledgement is made of the previous biography of Bruce by Robert Neal Rudmose Brown, *A Naturalist at the Poles* (1923), which provided a useful source of information that has been brought up-to-date in the light of recent research. In addition, a personal reminiscence of Bruce, given to the author by Bruce's daughter Sheila Mackenzie Bruce in 1992 (Sheila died in the mid 1990s), has provided invaluable background material.

My grateful thanks are due to Harry King, for many years librarian at the Scott Polar Research Institute (SPRI), Cambridge, and an internationally-acclaimed polar historian, for writing the foreword to this book. Special thanks are also due to the present librarian, William Mills, and to the SPRI archivist, Robert Headland, for allowing me access to the extensive documentary resources at the institute, and to the director, Professor Julian Dowdeswell, for permission to quote from them. Many thanks too to Anne Shirley (Savours), polar historian and writer, for her interest and enthusiasm. I am also indebted to Geoff Swinney, National Museums of Scotland, and professional associate of the Royal Scottish Geographical Society, for his interest, and for sharing the results of recent research. Other interested Scottish correspondents include Angus Erskine of Edinburgh and Peter Wordie of Dunblane, J A Gibson of *The Scottish Naturalist*, and Christine Simm, librarian of the Public Library in Bo'ness who was particularly interested in the work of Bruce and the Scottish Spitsbergen Syndicate. Professor Tony Hawkins, director of The Marine Laboratory, Aberdeen, brought me up-to-date with the activities of *Scotia III*, the new Fisheries research vessel.

I must also thank Lesley A Taylor and the staff of NMS Publishing at the National Museums of Scotland, for seeing the book safely through printing and publishing.

Peter Speak
November 2002

PICTURE CREDITS

THE photographs and illustrations in this book are by necessity black and white as they have been reproduced principally from original photographic negatives and glass plates. They have been sourced and are used by courtesy of the Scott Polar Research Institute (SPRI) (*pages* 1, 4, 20, 22, 62, 63, 69, 80, 83, 84, 93, 101, 127; see also art section); Royal Scottish Geographical Society (RSGS) (*pages* 54, 55, 76, 85, 94-5, 103, 106-7, 111; see also art section); Edinburgh University Library (EUL) (*pages* 44, 98, 100; see also art section); McManus Galleries, Dundee Council Leisure & Arts (*pages* 29, 32-3); Glasgow University Archive (*pages* 87, 93); and the Met Office (*pages* 42-3). I am also indebted to David Blight of St Austell for the rare picture of a group of Challenger office assistants (*page* 26); and similarly to Peter Wordie for the picture of members of the *Scotia* Expedition aboard ship (*page* 81); and to Sheila Mackenzie Bruce for family photographs and some personal letters. The source of each illustration and can be found in the caption line below each picture. Any pictures not attributed are in the author's possession. The track charts and maps (*pages* 10, 30, 110; see also art section) were drawn by Melanie Legge, cartographer in the geography department of Anglia Polytechnic University, Cambridge, and are used with permission.

FOREWORD

SOME eighty years have passed since the death of William Speirs Bruce, leader of eleven expeditions to Arctic Regions and two to the Antarctic. Of these the best known was the Scotia Expedition of 1902-04 which, coinciding as it did with Captain Robert Falcon Scott's Discovery Expedition, enjoyed little of the latter's publicity, notwithstanding Bruce's innovative oceanographical exploration of the Weddell Sea and his discovery of Coats Land.

The scientific results of the Scotia Expedition, covering the fields of physics, zoology and botany, were duly published in six volumes between 1907 and 1920. The first volume, numbered one in the series and entitled *The Log of the Scotia*, was held back from publication by Bruce's perennial shortage of ready cash. After Bruce's death the Log remained unpublished until, many years later, it surfaced among the Bruce papers in the archives of the Scott Polar Research Institute in Cambridge. It was discovered there by Peter Speak, then a research associate of the Institute, and published by Edinburgh University Press in 1992, prefaced by a short biography of Bruce.

Fortunately for scholarship Bruce had carefully hoarded the bulk of his papers and a collection was brought to Cambridge in 1947 by James Mann Wordie, a fellow Scot and at that time chairman of the Institute's committee of management.

While combing through the material, Peter Speak brought to light correspondence between Bruce and such close friends and associates as the climatologist Hugh Robert Mill and botanist Robert Neal Rudmose Brown, in addition to Bruce's arch antagonist Clements Robert Markham who was president of the Royal Geographical Society. All of this, along with other archival treasures, engendered in the mind of Peter Speak the concept of a new and revised 'life' of Bruce to take the place of Rudmose Brown's much earlier biography, *A Naturalist at the Poles,* published in 1923, only two years after Bruce's death. This ambition has now been realised in this volume.

In the concluding chapter the author reminds the reader that no plaque nor statue has yet been raised to commemorate Bruce's contribution to polar science and discovery and (as a fervent Scottish nationalist) his ardent desire that Scotland's place in the history of exploration would be forever recognised. This biography, together with *The Log of the Scotia*, should ensure that the name of William Speirs Bruce will at last receive the public recognition that has so long been denied him.

Harry G R King
former Librarian
SCOTT POLAR RESEARCH INSTITUTE
October 2002

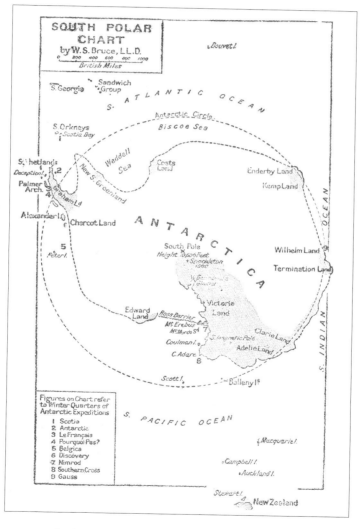

Bruce's own South Polar chart (taken from *Polar Exploration*, 1911).

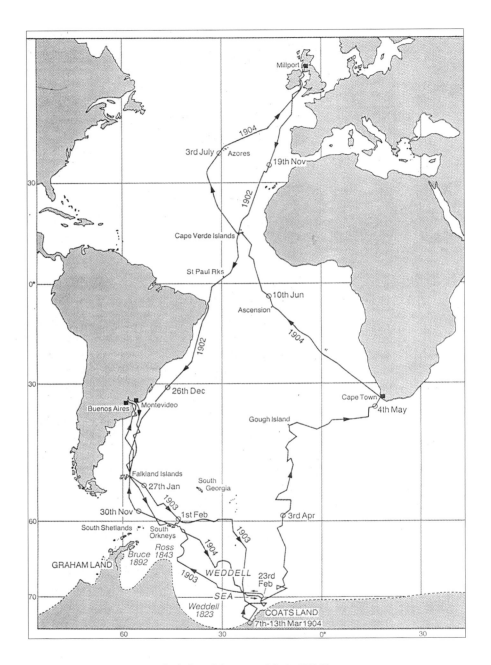

Track chart of the voyage of *Scotia*, 1902-04.

INTRODUCTION

IN the late morning of Sunday 2 November 1902 a sleek, ice-strengthened steam yacht named *Scotia* cast off her moorings in Troon harbour and headed out into the estuary of the River Clyde. On board were 26 officers and crew, and the seven scientists of the Scottish National Antarctic Expedition under the leadership of William Speirs Bruce.

As befitting an expedition planned, financed and recruited almost entirely from Scotland, the Lion Rampant and the Saltire flew from *Scotia*'s mast-heads. The expedition's official piper, Gilbert Kerr, played 'Auld Lang Syne', and the crew sang as the ship sailed out into the main channel. They were bound for the most treacherous region of the south polar ocean, the Weddell Sea, having signed on for 'a voyage from Troon to S. Polar Regions calling at any ports or places required on a voyage of discovery & scientific research, the voyage not to exceed 3 years'.

That Scotland had succeeded in mounting its own Antarctic expedition was a matter of considerable pride to Bruce. Around the turn of the century there had been substantial interest from many countries in the exploration of the little-known regions of the south. As his scientific colleagues on the expedition observed:

> *Germany, Sweden, and England, and later France, each had its own expedition, several of them largely aided by Government support. It remained for Scotland to show that as a nation her old spirit was still alive, and that she could stand beside the other nations and worthily take her place in this campaign of peace. It was in this spirit that the Scottish National Antarctic Expedition was planned and carried through by its indefatigable leader, Mr William S. Bruce.*

In 1897-99 a Belgian team, under Adrien de Gerlache, had explored the South Shetland Islands in the ship *Belgica*; in 1898-1900 Carsten Borchgrevink, a Norwegian under private British patronage, led the British Antarctic Expedition aboard *Southern Cross* and claimed to be the first to winter on the Antarctic continent; the German South Polar Expedition left Kiel in 1901 in *Gauss* under the leadership of Erich von Drygalski; and the Swedish South

Polar Expedition voyaged south in the same year in *Antarctic* under the direction of Nils Otto Nordenskjöld.

All these expeditions attempted only short journeys across the ice-covered continent and carried out, with varying degrees of success, limited scientific measurements and the collection of biological and geological specimens. Indeed the only expedition with a primary objective to pioneer a route to the South Pole was the 1901–04 British National Antarctic Expedition. This expedition, led by the Royal Navy officer Captain Robert Falcon Scott aboard *Discovery*, was the first to carry out extensive exploration on land in Antarctica while carrying out topographical surveying and scientific work.

For William Speirs Bruce and the Scottish National Antarctic Expedition, however, there was to be no time spent on an assault on the Pole. The Scotia voyage was planned as an oceanographical and meteorological expedition, and the ship was equipped with laboratories in which biological and geological specimens could be stored and preliminarily analysed. On board were the best sounding-devices, trawls, dredges and meteorological equipment available. It was an elaborate field excursion in polar natural history.

Bruce's aim was to establish a polar base in as high a latitude as possible and explore inland only as time allowed. He did not intend, unlike other national expeditions, that his ship should become frozen in the ice during the winter months in locations where a scientific programme would be severely limited. Nevertheless, because of delays caused by lack of funding, Bruce was forced to amend his plans. *Scotia* was overwintered in a sheltered bay of Laurie Island in the South Orkneys (60°S). A meteorological observatory was constructed and the zoology of the bay was studied by operating dredges through holes in the ice.

When spring finally released *Scotia* from the ice, after refit she sailed south into the eastern parts of the Weddell Sea where hitherto unknown lands were discovered (named Coats Land after the principal sponsors of the expedition). The ship finally returned home in 1904 after one of the most successful of all polar scientific expeditions, with no loss of life other than that of the chief engineer, Allan Ramsay, who tragically died from a chronic heart condition and was buried on Laurie Island.

Despite the success of the expedition in scientific terms, Bruce was aware that this was not enough to win popular support for future ventures. He wrote in the only book he prepared for the general public, *Polar Exploration* (1911):

> ... *what the mass of the public desire is pure sensationalism, therefore the polar explorer who attains the highest latitude and who has the powers of making a vivid picture of the difficulties and hardships involved will be regarded popularly as a hero and will seldom fail to add materially to his store of worldly welfare; while*

he who plods an unknown tract of land or sea and works there in systematic and monographic style will probably not have such worldly success ....

For Bruce this statement was to hold true for all his polar activities, whether in the Arctic or Antarctic, for this was the so-called Heroic Age of Polar Exploration and Bruce was not a typical hero of his time.

The period defined as the Heroic Age of Polar Exploration is a matter for debate. Vivian Fuchs wrote in his foreword to Bruce's *Log of the* Scotia *Expedition, 1902-4* (editor, Peter Speak), 'what is generally regarded as the Heroic Age of Antarctic Exploration may be considered to extend from 1900 to perhaps 1916'. The Rev. J Gordon Hayes, on the other hand, defined the 'Era' in *The Conquest of the South Pole: Antarctic Exploration 1906-1931* as beginning with the return to London of Captain Robert Falcon Scott from the Discovery Expedition in 1904, and ending with the flights over the Antarctic plateau and the South Pole by the Americans Rear-Admiral Richard E Byrd and Sir Hubert Wilkins in 1928 and 1929.

For the purposes of book, the Heroic Age is taken as 1895-1916, beginning in 1895 with the Sixth International Geographical Congress in London, where it was affirmed that 'the exploration of the Antarctic Regions is the greatest piece of geographical exploration still to be undertaken' and the constituent 'scientific societies throughout the world should urge in whatever way seems to them most effective, that this work should be undertaken before the close of the century'. By 1916 the Heroic Age was effectively over, with the safe return of Ernest Henry Shackleton's Imperial Trans-Antarctic Expedition following the crushing of *Endurance* in the ice, and the subsequent epic journey by sledge and open boat to South Georgia.

The Heroic Age was characterised by dramatic acts of personal achievement, such as Fridtjof Nansen's pioneering Arctic expedition aboard *Fram* in search of the North Pole (1893-96), the ill-fated attempt to reach the North Pole in 1897 by Swedish balloon aeronauts Saloman August Andrée, Nils Strindberg and Knut Fraenkel, two Antarctic expeditions led by Captain Scott (1901-04; 1911-13), the successful conquest of the South Pole by Roald Amundsen (1912), and two expeditions under the leadership of Ernest Shackleton (1907-09; 1914-16).

Individuals were ready, and even expected by the public eager for tales of adventure, to face inhospitable conditions of climate and terrain, often ill-prepared for such journeys into the unknown, and to cope with prolonged absence from home without basic communication. In Edwardian Britain, Captain Scott and and Ernest Shackleton epitomised the ideal heroic figure.

In the search for new lands in the south and the conquest of the South Pole, many scientific societies tried to persuade their Governments to raise national expeditions to carry the flag to Antarctica and there to make claim to new territory. Where reluctance was encountered to commit Government resources to exploratory projects and make them official, funds were often made available to supplement those raised by private donations. Thus in Britain polar expeditions were permitted to use the titles 'National' or 'Imperial', though mostly backed by private entrepreneurs or societies. In return it was understood that any territorial claims would be in the name of the Crown.

Scott and Shackleton excelled at promoting their work, which helped to raise funds from public and private sources alike to mount further expeditions. Bruce, on the other hand, despite having some powerful and influential friends, lacked the charisma of the other explorers. His shy, solitary nature made him a poor self-publicist, and his methodical and meticulous kind of scientific exploration did not deliver the sensational stories craved by the popular press. Thus without the ability to secure enough sponsorship, many of his ambitious plans for polar research had to be curtailed or abandoned.

Whereas the adventures of Scott and Shackleton are well documented in the popular annals of polar history, Bruce's contribution has largely been forgotten, despite the fact that he made two expeditions to the Antarctic and no fewer than eleven to Arctic regions. The Scottish National Antarctic Expedition was by far the most cost-effective and carefully planned scientific expedition of the Heroic Age and has been acknowledged by the eminent oceanographer Professor Tony Rice as 'fulfilling a more comprehensive programme than that of any previous or contemporary Antarctic expedition'.

Ironically it was this success that in part resulted in Bruce's lack of celebrity status, for he was first and foremost a scientist not a daring adventurer. In the early part of his career, he seemed even dismissive of headline-grabbing dashes to the Pole and those who advocated such attempts –

To reach the North Pole or South Pole is an athletic feat which may be put on the same level as an olympic race or gymnastic performance. It is not serious scientific work and can not in itself benefit mankind.

– and he grew increasingly bitter that those whose actions might be considered reckless attracted popular fame and, more importantly, funding to pursue further ventures.

It did not help that Bruce managed to alienate some very influential people, notably Clements Robert Markham, secretary to the Royal Geographical Society (also principal host of the International Geographical Congress in 1895). Markham, a powerful figure within the London scientific societies and well known to the Government, took charge of the organisation of the British National Antarctic Expedition of 1901–04. Bruce was by far the most experienced polar scientist in Britain at this time and he applied for a post on the British expedition (later known as the Discovery Expedition), but failed to receive even the courtesy of a reply from Markham for over a year. In frustration Bruce set about organising his own expedition. Markham was angered by the fact that Bruce's plans for a Scottish Antarctic expedition, supported by the Royal Scottish Geographical Society, would divert attention and sponsorship from the British expedition, and called the plans north of the border a 'mischievous rivalry'. He even spurned Bruce's offer to co-operate in a joint survey of Antarctic waters. (Bruce had suggested that *Scotia* would take the Weddell Sea quadrant, leaving *Discovery* to the Ross Sea quadrants, and the German ship *Gauss* under Erich von Drygalski to the remaining sector.) The Discovery Expedition eventually sailed in 1901 under the leadership of Captain Robert Falcon Scott.

Bruce's men went on to complete a highly successful expedition, but as a result of Markham's intransigence Bruce's endeavours in the field of polar exploration received little support from the London-based establishment. The Government, having already contributed substantially to the British Antarctic Expedition, had refused to offer funds for a rival Scottish venture, and Bruce had to fight for even a modest subsidy to support the publication costs of the scientific results. In an article entitled 'Scotland and Antarctica' (1908) written for *Scotia*, the journal of the St Andrew Society, Bruce was obviously still smarting from the lack of support:

A few weeks ago a letter appeared in the public press calling attention to the relative support the Scottish and English expeditions had from the British Government, and it was shown there that as usual the English got the money and the Scots got the kicks.

Bruce also attributed his failure to persuade the Royal Geographical Society to award the prestigious Polar Medal to members of the Scotia Expedition to opposition based on national prejudice. He applied many times, even raising the matter through Scottish Members of Parliament, but to no avail. Friends in London, however, quietly believed that he was too insistent, difficult in argument, and without the political guile to succeed. Even his life-long friend, the artist William Gordon Burn Murdoch, described Bruce as being 'as prickly as the Scottish thistle itself'.

Although science was the focus of his work, Bruce's passion for Scotland was an important aspect of his character. Bruce was born in 1867 in London's West End of a Welsh mother and a Scottish father. However, during summer vacation courses in natural history at the University of Edinburgh in 1887, taught by G F Scott Elliot and John Arthur Thomson, the young Bruce came under the influence of the course organiser, the inspirational naturalist and sociologist Professor (later Sir) Patrick Geddes, and felt increasingly compelled to make Scotland his homeland. Geddes was a central figure in a romantic Scottish renascence that aimed, as Rudmose Brown commented in his biography of Bruce, 'to awaken the dormant Celtic spirit, to rekindle the national fire and to show what Scotland could do in various walks of life'. In general this nationalism was largely cultural, expressed in literature and art, but Bruce, the scientist, embraced it wholeheartedly and it awoke in him a strong identification with his Scottish roots.

Whilst Bruce acknowledged the force of British Imperialism and accepted that British explorers would be in the vanguard of any polar exploration, he saw no conflict in independent Scottish initiatives running parallel to any originating in England. Bruce wished to see Scotland on an equal footing with England in a federal Britain at the heart of the Empire:

> Scotland is not a dependent country, but an individual nation working hand in hand on at least an equal footing with her partners in the Great British Federation. Scotland must acknowledge no predominant partner. Let her co-operate by all means, but if she is to have national existence she must be dictated to by no other nation, be it England, Russia or any other. An independent kingdom she has been, an independent kingdom let her remain. If by co-operation she is robbed by an Imperial Treasury let her have her own Treasury, if by co-operation she is robbed of her proper parliamentary representation, let her have her own parliament, if by co-operation she is robbed of her king and court, and her palaces are left desolate, let her have her own king. In short, in things which concern her integrity as a nation, Scotland must have absolute right to decide for herself.

Bruce came to see his treatment at the hands of an English-dominated establishment, as he perceived it, as a microcosm of Scotland's domination by England.

When it came to re-naming the Norwegian whaler *Hekla* after its refit in Troon in readiness for the Scottish Antarctic voyage, Bruce chose *Scotia,* the old name for Scotland. And after Markham's accusation of 'mischievous rivalry', Bruce altered the title of his venture from Scottish Antarctic Expedition to Scottish *National* Antarctic Expedition and he consciously set out to recruit most of the officers and crew from Scotland. The majority of the scientists had Scottish connections, and a substantial part of the funds came from Scottish benefactors large and small, with one or two notable exceptions. For Bruce the expedition was proof of Scotland's interest and expertise in polar scientific enquiry, a scientific contribution to the Scottish cultural renascence promoted by Geddes, and sufficient justification of the enterprise as a whole. As Bruce later noted in his preface to *The Voyage of the Scotia,* 'While "Science" was the talisman of the Expedition, "Scotland" was emblazoned on its flag'.

Despite the success of the Scotia Expedition, Bruce's name quickly faded from public memory even in his beloved Scotland. The value of his work and experience, however, was always recognised by specialists in the field of polar research, and by those who acted as mentors and colleagues over the years. Patrick Geddes was a major influence on Bruce, not just in the awakening of his feelings of nationalism, but also in his scientific career. Geddes caused him to change university and enroll as a medical student at Edinburgh. He also instilled in the young Bruce a multidisciplinary approach to the study of the natural environment, and in his expeditions Bruce's work was to include oceanography, hydrography, meteorology, zoology and cartography.

Geddes and his wife attracted about them a group of young people, mainly students, "Geddes' devoted disciples and servitors". Bruce, rather a loner, was on the fringes of this group, but through it met many of the brightest young thinkers in Edinburgh. Amongst them was Hugh Robert Mill. A few years after Bruce settled in Edinburgh, Mill moved to London to take up the influential position of librarian to the Royal Geographical Society, and he remained clearly impressed by the 'young medical student ... whom [he] knew as a shy, modest fellow, with an overmastering passion for collecting specimens of Natural History'. Mill initiated Bruce's move from medicine to polar research by recommending him for places on expeditions both to the Antarctic and the Arctic.

On Mill's recommendation, Bruce first journeyed to the Antarctic Peninsula as a naturalist and surgeon on *Balaena* with the Dundee Whaling Expedition of 1892-93. On his return he was recommended by Mill's colleague A J Herbertson (a future Professor of Geography at Oxford) for work at the Ben Nevis summit station, gaining further useful experience in meteorology and polar-like conditions. In the summer of 1896 he was invited to join, as zoologist, the Jackson-Harmsworth Expedition to Franz Josef Land; and in 1898 he returned to the Arctic on Andrew Coats' yacht *Blencathra*, sailing to Novaya Zemlya. On his way back from this expedition, Bruce had a chance meeting with Prince Albert of Monaco, one of the most respected oceanographers of the day. Impressed by Bruce's knowledge and enthusiasm, Albert invited him to join his Arctic expeditions and gave Bruce the opportunity to work with some of Europe's best ocean scientists and to use the most modern scientific equipment available. The experience proved invaluable to Bruce when planning his own future expeditions.

After the Scottish National Antarctic Expedition, Bruce worked towards a new project. Just as the circum-global Challenger Expedition of 1872-76 had made Edinburgh the centre for oceanography in the latter part of the nineteenth century, so Bruce tried to revive the city's pre-eminent position in that science by establishing the Scottish Oceanographical Laboratory in the premises adjacent to Surgeon's Hall in 1907. This provided a home for the vast collections of zoological and geological specimens brought back from his various expeditions, but also provided a base from which he could compile and publish the results of his researches. The laboratory also housed the various pieces of oceanographical apparatus that Bruce had amassed and interested individuals were welcome to seek advice or borrow equipment. As another of Bruce's life-long friends, Robert Neal Rudmose Brown, noted: 'In the cellars there was nearly all the equipment for a polar expedition from deep-sea trawls to teacups.'

The laboratory also witnessed the first meetings of the Scottish Ski Club. Bruce had been one of the first to ski in Scotland and had used skis both as a form of transport and for recreation during his expeditions. He was voted founder president of the club. The premises were also used for some of the early planning meetings for the Edinburgh Zoological Gardens and Bruce was one of the Zoological Society of Scotland's founder members.

Bruce had envisaged that the laboratory would be taken over by the University of Edinburgh and become a major international institute dedicated to the study of the world's oceans, much as the institute established by Albert of Monaco in Monte Carlo and Paris had become. Sadly this did not happen and, due to lack of funds, the laboratory was forced to close in 1919 shortly before Bruce's death. The collections were distributed between the University of Edinburgh, the Royal Scottish Geographical Society and the Royal Scottish Museum (later part of the National Museums of Scotland).

As a student in Edinburgh, Bruce had assisted John Murray in sorting, cataloguing and administering the vast collections brought back from the Challenger Expedition. The expedition had made John Murray, one of the naturalists on board, an extremely wealthy man as, after observing mineral-rich deposits of guano on some Pacific islands, he had established a company to extract phosphates of lime from Christmas Island.

Although scornful of expeditions seeking commercial reward, Bruce may have tried to emulate Murray's entrepreneurial success by applying his own geographical and scientific expertise to the exploitation of the mineral and landscape resources of the sub-Arctic islands now called Svalbard (the entire archipelago was known as Spitsbergen at that time). In 1909 Bruce launched the Scottish Spitsbergen Syndicate, a mineral prospecting company, offering shares for sale in the company. Although the work was primarily aimed at mineral exploitation, Bruce had reason to believe that oil and natural gas in particular might be discovered in economic quantities. Thus encouraged he made five visits to the Spitsbergen archipelago from 1909-20 on the Syndicate's behalf. In fact no oil or natural gas were ever found and the company, having failed to make any shareholder a fortune, was eventually sold in 1952.

Bruce also attempted to raise another Antarctic expedition from Scotland

in 1909-10. Too late he had recognised the need for spectacular achievements to woo sponsors and this time his plans included a trek right across
Antarctica via the South Pole. Unfortunately he failed to gain the funding,
but in 1914 Shackleton, aboard *Endurance*, set out to follow a broadly similar
route.

The ongoing work on the publication of the Scotia scientific results,
combined with the expense of running the laboratory, had been a constant
drain on Bruce's finances. Rudmose Brown noted: 'The pity is that Bruce was
a better hand at spending money than at making it: but all his schemes were
for the advancement of science; his own interests counted not at all.'

It was certainly shortage of money that prompted Bruce to accept an offer
from his old friend Burn Murdoch in 1915-16 to manage a whaling station in
the Seychelles. Although the station proved moderately successful in catching
and processing whales, the restrictions on trade as a result of World War I
resulted in the business going into liquidation within a year. Bruce came
back to Britain and offered his services to HM Government. Despite his vast
experience, he was disappointed to be offered only a minor position in the
Admiralty in London, preparing navigation manuals.

By 1920 Bruce was largely a broken man. Although only in his early
fifties, the hardships he had endured in pursuit of his science had taken their
toll and his physical and mental health were failing. When he joined the
Syndicate's summer expedition to Spitsbergen in 1920, he was not able to
contribute much to the work and went along largely as a passenger. He died
in 1921.

Although the achievements of William Speirs Bruce rank high in the
Heroic Age of Polar Exploration, he is now a forgotten hero. His golden
years were undoubtedly between 1892 and 1907 when the promise of his
youth was realised. However, lacking the charisma of his contemporary
explorers, Bruce remained focussed throughout his life on science rather than
publicity, and he was often unbending in his approach.

There is no public memorial to his name, although the collections he
amassed and the archive of documents left behind give a vivid impression
of man who, for a brief period early in the twentieth century, almost single-
handedly put Scotland at the forefront of polar research. Through his
dedication to science, Bruce made a major contribution to our knowledge
of the polar regions of the globe, a contribution made with considerable
self-sacrifice. When, in the autumn of 1902, Bruce departed for a period
'not to exceed 3 years' aboard *Scotia,* he left behind his wife Jessie and their
son who was barely seven months old. This, and subsequent long absences,
put inevitable strain on their marriage.

In a letter to Bruce in 1912, Patrick Geddes, instrumental in guiding Bruce
towards environmental research, summarised Bruce's contribution:

William Speirs Bruce flies the Saltire over his camp at Spitsbergen. (*SPRI*)

For not only have you been the actual initiator of this now world-wide movement of Antarctic Exploration, but also its most enduring and most effective scientific votary. You have necessarily sacrificed the world-wide attention and interest earned by more dramatic expeditions for the steady, though not the less dangerous labour of Antarctic Survey in all its details, oceanic and abyssal, terrestrial, meteorological, magnetic, biological &c .... Your observations thus constitute a body of scientific matter which I believe to be unparalleled in its completeness and range, and its consequent value and example. It is thus by no mere local patriotism that you should be supported; but rather by the mass of scientific workers over the world.

Echoing the sentiments of Patrick Geddes, the aim of this book is to celebrate the centenary of Bruce's finest achievement, the Scottish National Antarctic Expedition, and to recall for a modern readership the outstanding qualities and achievements of one of Scotland's finest polar explorers and scientists who carried the Saltire, with little reward, to some of the most inhospitable environments of the Earth.

References

Bruce, William Speirs: *The Log of the* Scotia *Expedition, 1902-4* (editor, Peter Speak) (Edinburgh: Edinburgh University Press, 1992).

Bruce, William Speirs: *Scottish National Antarctic Expedition: Report on the Scientific Results of the Voyage of SY Scotia during the years 1902, 1903, and 1904* (Edinburgh, 1907–20), vols II–VII.

Rudmose Brown, Robert Neal: *A Naturalist at the Poles* (London, 1923).

Three of the Staff: *The Voyage of the Scotia* (Edinburgh, 1906) [new edition with introduction by David Munro, Edinburgh: Mercat Press, 2002].

CHAPTER 1

THE EARLY YEARS

WILLIAM Speirs Bruce may have been denied a Scottish nationality by birth, but he was to become the foremost of Scotland's polar explorers and scientists and a fervent nationalist.

Bruce, on his father's side, was descended from an Orcadian family, the Isbisters. His grandfather (born in Glasgow in 1799) was the Rev. William Bruce. He married Charity Isbister and converted to the newly-fashionable Swedeborgian Church in the 1820s, becoming an assistant to Thomas Parker, the leader of the Church in Edinburgh. William gave up a brief spell as a schoolmaster to attend to his pastoral duties and moved to the New Church in Dundee where, at the age of 30, he was ordained as its minister. The Rev. Bruce later moved to take over the Church in Edinburgh before moving to London in 1851, where he ministered at a church of the same faith in Cross Street in the prosperous district of Hatton Gardens. There he succeeded the incumbent, the Rev. Samuel Noble. William Bruce eventually resigned from his ministerial post on the grounds of ill health in 1861, but continued to preach occasionally and edited the journal *Intellectual Repository*.

When William and Charity's first son was born (in Edinburgh), he was christened Samuel Noble Bruce. He grew up in London and was educated at University College School, later becoming a doctor. Samuel's medical practice was established in the middle-class district of Knightsbridge, West London.

Samuel married Mary Lloyd (known in the family as Sara), the daughter of L Wild Lloyd, an architect. After they married they lived in Queensberry Terrace and then moved not far away to Kensington Gardens Square. It was here, at number 43, that their children were born and lived in comparative prosperity.

William Speirs Bruce was born on 1 August 1867. Although on his birth certificate his father's profession is given as 'surgeon', he would today be called a general practitioner. Evidently he was very successful in his practice, as he and his wife were not only able to raise a family of eight children, but also to support his father and sister – as well as a retinue of servants, coachmen and nursemaids. The family later moved to an even more prestigious middle-

Samuel Noble Bruce, father, and the young William Speirs Bruce. *(SPRI)*

class address, 18 Royal Crescent, Holland Park, where, according to Bruce's daughter Sheila, they had two horse-drawn carriages and employed two footmen, as well as several general servants.

William Speirs was the fourth child of eight and the elder of two sons. He was given his distinctive middle name after another branch of the family in Scotland. Unfortunately its spelling has been the source of repeated error. Even his great friend and companion on *Scotia*, Rudmose Brown, a biologist and geographer, consistently mis-spelled his name in his biography of Bruce, *A Naturalist at The Poles* (1923). The mistake – 'Spiers' for 'Speirs' – has been repeated in articles and books on exploration ever since. At other times 'Spears' has appeared. Bruce, who was meticulous in all things, was very sensitive to the correct rendering of his family name and complained bitterly about its misuse.

Although Bruce enjoyed a comfortable early life, according to his granddaughter Moira Watson, now living in Hamilton, Ontario, his father was somewhat tyrannical and Bruce maintained a distant relationship with him after moving to Scotland. When Samuel retired from medical practice and remarried a former patient after the death of his first wife, his children, now adults, were already living away from home. On learning of his son's death at the comparatively early age of 54, Samuel expressed surprise at the extent and importance of his son's considerable contribution to polar research.

However, Bruce writes fondly of other members of the family, his sisters in particular. Only William Speirs and his brother Douglas had children (each a son and daughter), and only the former pursued an academic career. Douglas was sent to California in his late teens to work on an orange grove, and for some time in the inter-war years he managed a farm, rearing rabbits. Four of the sisters became nurses (no doubt encouraged by their father), including Violet and the eldest sister Mary. Eveline entered a religious order in Germany before World War I and became a nursing sister, but her father used his influence with the British authorities to bring her home in the early days of the war, much to Eveline's regret. She had taught English to Queen Mary's sister, the Duchess of Teck, and was a highly-respected individual. The other sisters were Monica, an artist specialising in watercolour painting, who lived in Cornwall; and Mabel, who married Alec Welch, one-time editor of the *Strand Magazine*. The youngest daughter, Isobel, also became a nurse, working at Waterloo in London and later taking over the running of the house in Holland Park after her father retired.

This was the family background of William Speirs Bruce; not particularly remarkable in its ambitions nor attainments, and not especially favourable for an aspiring polar explorer. However, one factor might have contributed to his later career. Samuel Bruce wrote to Rudmose Brown shortly after Bruce's death in 1921, commenting on his son's early days in London:

> *In looking back over my son's boyhood I find hardly any outstanding events to record such as might give early signs of the strenuous and steadfast character of his mature life.*
>
> *My father and sister were almost the sole teachers, as they were the chief companions of the children, and it was their daily custom to go out with them into Kensington Gardens, which were near, and sometimes into the Natural History Museum, which was not far off. To these influences is due, as I think, his interest in life and nature.*

This could well have been the start needed by one who was destined to devote most of his life to natural history. The study of the subject had also been invigorated by the publication of Charles Darwin's *On the origin of species, by means of natural selection: or the preservation of favoured traits in the struggle for life* in 1859; and museums were being built in many major towns and cities throughout the country to house in part the collections of natural history specimens inspired by this age of popular science.

Bruce's formal education began, however, when he was sent to a progressive boarding school in 1879 at the age of twelve, the Norfolk County School in the small market town of North Elmham. He remained there until 1885, the year after his grandfather, William, died.

Having passed the matriculation examination at his third attempt, Bruce was enrolled by his father at University College, London to study medicine, beginning in the autumn term of 1887. However, before the term started Bruce was sent on two summer courses in biology in Edinburgh.

For anyone with a latent interest in the natural sciences at that time, there was no better place to be in the whole of Britain than the city of Edinburgh. Scottish science and academic life in general were enjoying a golden period, comparable to that at the end of the previous century, and Bruce would have been surrounded by scientists of high intellectual calibre destined to become eminent in their chosen disciplines.

The first great voyage devoted to oceanographical science, the Challenger Expedition, had taken place between 1872 and 1876 and its collections were currently being managed and administered from a dedicated office in Queen Street, Edinburgh. Almost entirely Scottish in the composition of scientists and crew, the Challenger Expedition was led by Professor Wyville Thomson and commanded by Captain George Nares of the Royal Navy. They were later knighted for their services, as were the principal biologist John Murray and pioneer chemist John Young Buchanan.

Studies in the natural sciences were also very popular. At the University of Edinburgh eminent scholars such as P G Tait, John Arthur Thomson and William Turner, gave lecture courses in the subject that included anatomy and physiology; while other luminaries resident in the city included the founder of the British Meteorological Service, Alexander Buchan, and Bruce's mentor at the summer school, Patrick Geddes, leader of the holistic approach to environmentalism and a founder of present-day ecological studies. The young Bruce came under the influence of all these eminent scholars, some of whom were to become his advocates and close friends. Both Patrick Geddes and his wife, for example, remained close to Bruce for the rest of his life.

Geddes had organised two summer courses in natural science: one was on botany at the Royal Botanic Garden; the other on practical zoology. The latter took place at the Royal Scottish Marine Station, Granton and along the shores of the Firth of Forth, making use of an old canal barge called the *Elizabeth*, affectionately known as 'the *Ark*', for laboratory classes. The tutor, John Arthur Thomson, was a lecturer on zoology in the University of Edinburgh's school of medicine and a personal friend of Geddes.

Geddes was an expert in the fields of biology, sociology and geography, and later became well known as an ecologist and town planner. As an environmentalist he advocated a generalist approach, stressing the interaction of the sciences rather than specialising in any one of the branches of natural science. To an impressionable 20 year-old like Bruce, Geddes was an inspiring figure indeed.

Through the summer course Bruce not only learned the techniques of natural history investigation, but also met the foremost natural scientists of the day. This experience, arriving somewhat fortuitously, altered the direction of Bruce's career. Thereafter Scotland was to become his home and his passion; and the pursuit of natural history, especially in high latitudes, his principal goal.

Abandoning his father's plans for him to study medicine at University College, Bruce enrolled in the medical school at the University of Edinburgh instead. After several other places of residence he moved in 1891 to student halls in Riddle's Court, off the Royal Mile. Halls of residence, of which Riddle's Court was one, had been established by Geddes as an experiment in 'social living'. Just as Geddes the ecologist was fascinated by the *ecumene*, or community of plants and animals, so Geddes the sociologist was similarly fascinated by the human behaviour of young men in a student environment. An account of this period of William's life was included in Rudmose Brown's biography, contributed by Bruce's friend Burn Murdoch.

Bruce's student days appear to have been happy, but even then he demonstrated a characteristic seriousness of purpose and selfless devotion to science. He was rarely seen to smile and this was echoed in his personal demeanour. His 'clothes hung loosely on him and with his wide black eye-brows and hair, and with a slight stoop and his face, no-one could have believed what a wiry endurance he had'. He was physically very strong, for he could 'reel off a sixty-mile walk in a day without turning a hair' and 'at swimming he was hard to beat'.

Hugh Robert Mill, who came to know Bruce in these formative years, possibly through Geddes, described him as 'a shy gentle fellow with appealing eyes … always ready to do a kindness to anyone … his love of Nature was unusually strong. He was an ideal naturalist, quite unspecialised and equally interested in every phenomenon and form of life, a perfect type of the born naturalist.'

At the university, Bruce was receiving instruction in anatomy, biology and medicine, and at weekends, or whenever else he was free, he worked on specimens brought back by *Challenger* on its four-year voyage around the world, assisting in the laboratory under the tuition of John Murray and John Young Buchanan. In this capacity he would have had the opportunity to proof read articles in preparation for the Challenger reports and to meet and correspond with the best oceanographers of the day. This gave him valuable experience of scientific routines and the rigour of report writing. He was also learning to recognise the various systems of classification of biological and rock specimens and, given the opportunity to conduct his own oceanographic research, he would have been ready to collect specimens, enter field data in reports, and approach the experts in different fields of scientific knowledge to assess his findings.

Some of the Challenger office assistants. The original photograph was framed in wood from the mast of HMS *Challenger*. A young-looking William Speirs Bruce (left) sits cross-legged, unsmiling, on the studio floor. With characteristic reserve he signed himself 'W S Bruce', although the others have provided their first names. (*David Blight*)

The eminent scientist John Murray had been the senior biologist on *Challenger*. Between 1876, when the ship returned to Scotland, and 1895 when the last of the Challenger reports was published, Murray was chief editor. He was helped by young assistants in the arduous task of preparing the fifty volumes of reports for the press. The work was carried out principally in the Challenger office, located initially at 32 Queen Street, and later at 45 Frederick Street, Edinburgh.

Bruce was fascinated by the intellectual challenge of natural history and determined to make natural science his life's work. Since Darwinism had become accepted as an appropriate paradigm (or conceptual model) for the explanation of the origin of the diversity of living animals, examples and evidence were required from all parts of the world. Wealth had so increased during this industrial age that there were rich and influential amateurs willing to fund expeditions to the farthest ends of the Earth. Thus the prime reasons for Antarctic exploration at the start of the twentieth century were threefold: scientific, commercial and, increasingly, nationalistic.

Commerce and exploration, however, were combined for less philanthropic reasons. Who could say that *terra incognita* would not yield priceless raw materials, the stuff of industry? All Victorian and Edwardian expeditions, wherever they went, were expected to search for gold and other minerals and to survey the oceans for new fishing grounds. Scotland in particular was well favoured for this kind of quest in high latitudes – there were redundant whaling ships in the north-east coast harbours which could be chartered relatively cheaply to look for new grounds to replace those in Arctic waters, with masters and officers accomplished in ice navigation.

However, there was a further motive that complemented those of science and commerce – the complex motive of nationalism. Newly-discovered lands could be claimed for one's country and the successful explorer might be promoted in society and presented with prestigious awards. It would be naïve to believe that even polar explorers were immune to thoughts of self-aggrandisement.

For Bruce, however, polar science was to become his life's work; he would have no other profession. Apart from giving evening lectures in general geography at Heriot-Watt College, Edinburgh (1899-1901 and 1917-19), and at the Church of England Training College (1899-1901), a brief spell as a director and manager of a whaling company in the Seychelles (1915-16), and a year at the Admiralty during World War I, Bruce rarely experienced the security of regular paid employment.

References

Bruce, William Speirs: *The Log of the* Scotia *Expedition, 1902-4* (editor, Peter Speak) (Edinburgh: Edinburgh University Press, 1992).

Bruce, William Speirs: *Report on the Scientific Results of the Voyage of SY Scotia during the years 1902, 1903, and 1904* (Edinburgh, 1907-20), vols II-VII.

Linklater, Eric: *The Voyage of the Challenger* (London, 1974).

Moorehead, Alan: *Darwin and the Beagle* (Harmondsworth, 1969).

Rudmose Brown, Robert Neal: *A Naturalist at the Poles* (London, 1923).

Swinney, G N: 'The training of a polar scientist: Patrick Geddes and the student career of William Speirs Bruce' in *Archives of Natural History*, vol 29, pp 287-301 (2002).

CHAPTER 2

THE DUNDEE EXPEDITION

BY the middle of the nineteenth century it had become apparent to the northern whaling fleets that the population of whales in the North Atlantic was in serious decline. Over-fishing was almost certainly the reason. Whaling as an important commercial activity had been initiated at the end of the sixteenth century by merchants from Britain, France, the Netherlands, Norway and the Basque ports. In the seventeenth century the industry shifted westwards into waters around Jan Mayen and Iceland, and moved further west to Davis Strait between the west coast of Greenland and Baffin Island in the late eighteenth and early nineteenth centuries. By the 1870s many of the whaling ships were idle, but there was still a demand for whale oil and blubber, and particularly for baleen, the flexible filter plates from the jaws of certain whales. This was vital raw material for the manufacture of a variety of goods including umbrella spokes and corsets. Baleen from the jaws of a single whale could be worth as much as £2000–3000.

The whaling industry began to consider looking elsewhere for its catch and speculated on the possibilities of the Southern Ocean. It was known that Antarctic fur seals (*Arctocephalus gazella*) had been caught in the 1820s, even to the point of extinction, but there were no records of the capture of baleen whales despite reported sightings. In the Royal Naval Erebus and Terror Expedition to the Antarctic (1839-43), under the command of Captain (later Rear Admiral) James Clark Ross, a 'right' species of whale had been sighted. The right whale had huge baleen plates, was relatively slow in the water and, once harpooned, floated conveniently on the surface of the water instead of sinking to the bottom. It was, therefore, 'right' for capture and subsequent processing. This offered renewed hope to the industry that these whales might halt the decline of the whale fishing fleets off the east coast of Britain, from Peterhead in Scotland to Whitby in England.

In 1874 a report was published in Peterhead by the brothers David and John Gray, 'On The New Whaling Grounds in the Southern Seas', designed to stimulate interest in the fishing of Antarctic waters. The report was reprinted in Aberdeen in the same year, and in the journal of the Royal Society of Victoria in Melbourne, Australia in 1887, and again in 1891 in Peterhead.

The whaling ship *Balaena* berthed in Dundee Harbour. Note *Windward* in the background.
(McManus Galleries, Dundee City Council Leisure & Arts)

The Royal Scottish Geographical Society sent the pamphlet to the Royal Geographical Society of Australasia, and they, together with the Royal Society of Victoria, set up the Antarctic Exploration committee to propose and promote continued scientific and commercial work in this field.

German-born Baron Ferdinand von Muellern was an important supporter of these proposals. In his inaugural speech to the Royal Geographical Society in Melbourne on 18 April 1884, he suggested a joint venture between British and Australian interests. Financial backing was not forthcoming, however. Instead, an approach was made to three established whaling entrepreneurs: Robert Kinnes of Dundee, and the Norwegians Christien Christensen of Sandefjord and Svend Føyn of Tønsberg. This initiative led directly to the exploration of the Antarctic seas as potential whaling grounds.

In 1892 Kinnes had fitted out four whaling ships with auxiliary steam engines and a total crew of 130 to search for right whales in the Antarctic. The expenses of equipping the fleet came to £28,000. The ships were *Balaena* (under Captain Alexander Fairweather), *Active* (Captain Thomas Robertson), *Diana* (Captain Robert Davidson) and *Polar Star* (Captain James Davidson). *Balaena* was the largest: 260 tons register, 141 feet in length, 31 in the beam, draught 16½ feet (42.9 x 9.4 x 5 metres), with a 65hp engine. It was built originally at Drammen in Norway, under the name of *Mjolnar*, with its hull of timbers 32 inches (81cm) thick, specially designed for work in ice.

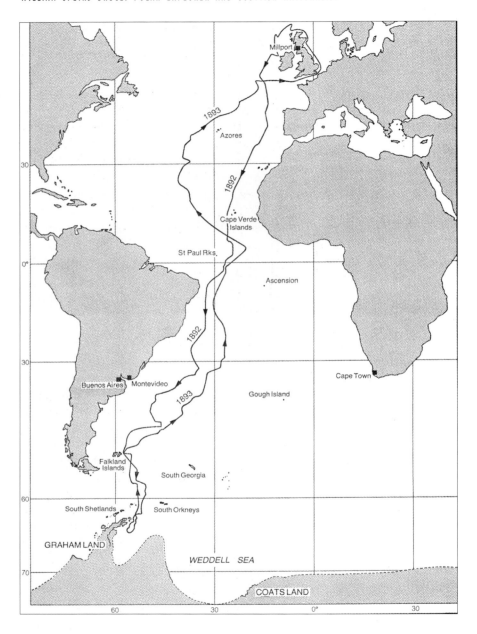

Track chart of the voyage of *Balaena*, 1892-1893.

The four ships left harbour in Dundee on 6 September 1892, heading for the Antarctic Peninsula. In his book *Life Interests of a Geographer, 1861-1944*, Hugh Robert Mill wrote:

> One of my first duties at the Royal Geographical Society had been to draw up a set of Instructions for Naturalists visiting the Antarctic Regions. Mr Leigh Smith was supplying nautical instruments to the captains of four Dundee whalers just returned 'clean' from the Arctic seas and determined to try their fortunes in the Antarctic. He had persuaded them to take out young naturalists as surgeons, and asked me if I could help. It was then that I thought of a young medical student, William Speirs Bruce, whom I knew as a shy, modest fellow, with an overmastering passion for collecting specimens of Natural History; and later I heard of [Charles] W Donald and others who were willing to go on the adventure. I was in Scotland when the four ships sailed, and I took Mr Andrew Coates of Perth with me to Dundee to bid farewell to Bruce in Balaena, (Captain Fairweather), and to C W Donald in the Active, (Captain Robertson). Half an hour before the ship sailed, Bruce lounged up. 'All ready,' he said. The steward asked him, 'Where is your bedding?' — the first intimation that he had to supply his own requirements in that respect. He appealed to me in despair — he had no money, and I had not enough to do any good; but Coates generously presented a five pound note, a bystander showed the way to the nearest ship-chandler's, and Bruce returned triumphant just in time.

At about the same time, Christensen in Norway despatched *Jason* under Carl Anton Larsen from Sandefjord. They reached the Western Weddell Sea on 23 December of that year. The ships explored the area of the Southern Ocean off the Antarctic Peninsula, South Sandwich Islands and South Orkneys before a rendezvous on Boxing Day when all five ships reported that they had not witnessed a single right whale. It was clear that the expedition was not going to plan.

William Gordon Burn Murdoch, an artist and good friend of Bruce (they met in Riddle's Court in 1891), shipped as assistant surgeon. Burn Murdoch brought back paintings and wrote a full account of the rather disappointing expedition in the book *From Edinburgh to the Antarctic* (1894). Bruce contributed chapter XIX (untitled) to the book, on the natural history of the Antarctic, describing the equipment on *Balaena*, its use, and the scientific observations, and the fact that he was entirely dependent on the goodwill of scientists and scientific bodies for his instruments. In a report to the Royal Geographical Society (*Geographical Journal*, vol 7, 1896), Bruce wrote:

> With the consent of the owners and masters the Royal Geographical Society spent over £150 in equipping these four vessels with instruments for geographical observation. The Meteorological Office provided a complete set of meteorological

The ships of the 1892-93 Dundee Whaling Expedition, from a painting by William Gordon Burn Murdoch. *(McManus Galleries, Dundee City Council Leisure & Arts)*

instruments. Mr Leigh Smith, who has done so much to enlarge our knowledge of the Arctic regions, extended his exploring interest to the Antarctic by adding to the Balaena's equipment a handsome outfit of biological apparatus, a deep-sea thermometer, etc. for my use. Professor Haddon contributed two deep-sea thermometers, and Dr. H R Mill a pocket aneroid and a spectroscope. The Active, the Diana, and the Polar Star were supplied by Professor D'Arcy Thompson with a zoological outfit, while he drew up a series of careful directions to guide us all in the collecting and preserving of natural history specimens.

Bruce and Burn Murdoch initially shared the small cabin allocated to Bruce, the only space left at the last minute. As friends they were able to support each other in this great new venture. However, while Bruce had some medical knowledge he could scarcely sustain the title of surgeon, and Burn Murdoch, having signed on at the pay of one shilling per month as Bruce's assistant, had no experience of medicine at all. Fortunately for them both, and for the crew of *Balaena,* there were no serious injuries or illnesses to attend to.

At this time it was customary to include in ships' crews both artists and naturalists. Although photography was developed by the 1890s, an artist could

add the dimension of colour to an illustration which otherwise would have been rendered in black and white. The artist's job was to draw and paint natural history specimens as well as capture the mood of sea and landscapes. The best known of such marine illustrators was Sir Joseph Hooker, who was taken by Ross on the Erebus and Terror Expedition and who later published the ground-breaking book *Flora Antarctica*. Burn Murdoch, with a few exceptions, seemed to have confined his work largely to shipboard sketches of the crew and their activities.

When it became obvious that there were no right whales in the areas of sea under investigation by the five ships, the order went out to cut their losses by filling the ships' holds with seal skins, seal oil and blubber. Seals were abundant and easy quarry, and since they were to be found on every island and group of rocks the crews were able to capture them on the ice with ease. In spite of their stated roles on the ship, both Bruce and Burn Murdoch were expected to share in the mass killing. Bruce hated it. He was prepared to kill for science, but slaughter for commercial gain appalled him.

The four Dundee ships and the Norwegian vessel returned to home ports with cargoes of seal oil and skins, but bearing a financial loss. For Bruce and Burn Murdoch in particular, there was sense of frustration that the commercial objectives of the expedition had dominated the scientific aspiration. Captain Fairweather had shown little interest in Bruce's work and even proposed selling his specimens of rocks, skins, eggs, *etc* on the Dundee quayside. However most ultimately found their way to specialists. Bruce wrote to Mill on 31 May 1893:

> *I am hourly awaiting the arrival of Mr Leigh Smith with whose intervention I hope there will be no difficulty in disposing of what material there is – which is a miserable show to what it should have been.*

Bruce was in Dundee on 21 June, possibly staying with Geddes who had a Chair in Botany at the University College that required him to live and work in Dundee during the summer term. It was here that Bruce met Rudmose Brown, one of Geddes' assistants. Here too he wrote the following *apologia* for the scientific work of the Dundee Expedition to the 'Secretaries of the Royal Geographical Society' in London as follows:

> *Although my report is not yet handed in, still as the limited extent of the collections and observations is already somewhat generally known, I think it well at this time to offer a word of explanation of the meagre results of my work, and my inexperience was not entirely to blame, as certainly my interest was not lacking.*
>
> *The general bearing of the master was far from being favourable to scientific work. Though not exactly forced to work in the boats, still I found it a practical necessity, while the re-iterated statement that the whole collection would belong to the ship doubtless also tended in some degree to allay my enthusiasm. Looking back over the voyage I can understand that the inevitable differences in point of view of skipper and naturalist may have been a mutual source of irritation, but I also may fairly claim not only to have been obedient to all commands, but even conciliatory to the best of my ability. I can say the same of my companion, Mr W G Burn Murdoch, and it is our united belief that if we have erred, it has not been by not asserting our respective claims and duties more firmly, but on board ship this is no easy matter.*
>
> *The objections made to obtaining occasional access to the charts and the almost total omission of solar observations and careful taking of bearings during our stay in the ice has made it impossible to locate accurately the various facts and phenomena.*
>
> *The sounding machine was used on rare occasions and then only for convenience sake.*
>
> *Meteorological observations while at the ice are very incomplete on account of my being constantly in the boats and having no assistance whatsoever given me in the watches necessary for rest.*
>
> *I was unfortunate enough to have my special bucket carried away by a sea on the 26th of December; the ship's buckets were unfit for obtaining pure water on account of their oily and dirty state, and were practically past cleansing, so that for the rest of*

the time in the ice the recording of surface salinities and temperatures was next to impossible.

Coming to the collections I was here especially unfortunate no accommodation being allowed me for their preparation. Bird specimens whether entire or as skins and skeletons, seals' skeletons, and rock specimens were all alike recklessly heaved overboard.

Tow netting was naturally impracticable when I was in the boats, and unsatisfactory also during heavy weather owing to the vast amount of seal refuse thrown overboard; many occasions however were lost owing to the strong feeling expressed against it, the alleged explanation being that it stopped the way of the ship. The majority of tow nettings on the passage home were in fact taken surreptitiously during the night and morning watches.

The box containing specimens of sea water was broken into and the bottles removed in spite of an officer of the ship.

From the outset I was fully conscious of my own imperfect preparation for such an expedition and I have of course learned this even more fully at different emergencies. I trust however to have learned much by the voyage and am now continuing my studies here in some of the departments of which I have most felt my limitations. I have to thank the Society for assisting me in what has been, despite all drawbacks, an instructive and delightful experience, and shall be hopeful if another opportunity be given me of bringing back larger results to the Society.

'Despite all drawbacks', Bruce was able to contribute a substantial paper to volume XII of the *Proceedings of the Royal Physical Society of Edinburgh*, entitled 'Animal Life Observed during a Voyage to Antarctica' (also published in the *Journal of the Manchester Geographical Society*, vol 10, 1894). In his paper Bruce commented upon the abundance of seals, noting the four species encountered as the sea leopard (*Hydrurga leptonyx*), Weddell's false sea leopard (*Leptonychotes weddellii*), the crab-eating seal (*Lobodon carcinophagus*) and Ross's large-eyed seal (*Ommatophoca rossii*). He observed the habits of the seals and the ease of capture thus:

In December all seals are in bad condition, thinly blubbered, and grievously scarred —, and during January their condition improved, and by February they were heavily blubbered and free of scars. Loving the sun they lie on the pack all day digesting their meal of the previous night, which had consisted of fish or small crustaceans, or both.

The present generation had never seen man, and at his approach, they did not attempt to flee, but surveyed him open-mouthed and fearful, during which process they were laid low with club or bullet.

Bruce never reconciled himself to mass slaughter and added:

While we continue to require sacks, while we persist in wearing patent leather shoes, and while we satisfy our fancies with certain purses and card-cases, the slaughter of these seals will continue. But I would publicly here protest against the indiscriminate massacre which takes place in order to supply blubber as well as hides, for the purpose indicated. Old and young, females with young, are slaughtered alike, and should this continue, these seals, like the Antarctic Fur Seals at the beginning of the century, will be exterminated.

[His views, 100 years ago, on the conservation of sea mammals, resonate sympathetically with the policies of conservationists today. Fortunately wise council and a changing economic situation did result in a more enlightened approach to seal culling in the next century.]

Bruce's initiation to the hard world of whaling ships, sea captains, and crewmen was salutary. He soon realised that his enthusiasm for the science of the natural world was unlikely to be shared by shipowners and their work-force whose primary, if not sole objectives, were commercial and pecuniary. He was a raw polar traveller and it was understandable that ships' crews, whose livelihoods were dependent on filling the holds with large catches of blubber, skins and oil, had little time for scientific experiment and recording.

However, in spite of the meagreness of the scientific results of the Dundee Expedition, Bruce was convinced of the importance of studies of polar marine and terrestrial environments to science. He had given up his under-graduate studies in order to join the expedition, and had no expectation of support from his family to fund sustained research in extremely remote and icy parts of the world. With no other qualifications that might earn him a living, he now found that he had to turn to richer friends, or academic and government institutions, for financial and material support.

Bruce wrote to Mill in June 1893, outlining his wish to go to the 'far South' this time, adding 'the taste I have had has made me ravenous'. In a letter written to Mill only five days later, he demonstrated his ambitions:

I have received a nice letter from Lady Goldsworthy, whom I think looks encouraging to the South Georgian scheme. This scheme I may tell you is far from being the only one I have on hand nor is it the chief. I have fairly definite ideas of a true Antarctic research expedition and look upon South Georgia as a stepping stone. I believe that more can be done in the south than the north and that many of the supposed terrors and impossibilities do not exist, and that the belief of their existence has simply arisen from want of knowledge of those parts. Were I to follow out my own inclinations I should launch forth immediately and endeavour to carry out some of my plans but I have to consider that my father's years are increasing, and that he finds the work he has to do too much for him, and consequently have to consider which is the best way I can assist him and the family in the future. It seems to me that too much money is expected for an expedition to the south and that very good work can be done with a far smaller sum, part of that sum if not the whole being covered by cargoes of a scientific nature – bones, skins, fossils, etc. for the museums of the world.

[Lady Goldsworthy was the wife of the Governor of the Falklands at that time and Bruce had met them both when *Balaena* had briefly called in at the Falklands on the return journey from the south. And Bruce's concern for his father, whilst commendable, proved misplaced as Bruce senior outlived him.]

Looking for support from the Royal Geographical Society, Bruce wrote from 3 Derby Street, Mayfair, London, on 22 August 1893 to Dr John Scott Keltie, secretary to the Society, enclosing plans for a return to the Antarctic:

I herewith enclose my suggestions for my proposed visit to South Georgia which you asked me to lay before the Council of the Society.

I should have proposed further investigation in more southern latitudes, viz. South Shetlands or Graham's Land, had I thought there had been any chance of my being landed there at the present time.

His outline of the proposed expedition to South Georgia was comprehensive, as this attached memorandum, written at University Hall, Edinburgh, suggests:

– *To complete, as far as possible, the Geographical Survey of the island of South Georgia.*
– *To note its Geological structure with due reference to its Mineralogy and Palaeontology.*
– *To take serial Meteorological observations, noting the general condition of the climate.*
– *To investigate the fauna and the flora, especially marine forms, and to make collections.*
– *To note how far the various Seal fisheries might be developed, and even the possibilities of again introducing fur seals, and encouraging them to remain by protection.*
– *To test the capabilities of the island for sheep, cattle, and crops.*

For the fulfilment of the above suggestions it will be necessary:

– *To have at least one Assistant, though more assistance if obtainable.*
– *To be provided with outfit, both Scientific and personal.*
– *To arrange specially for the passages between the Falkland Islands and South Georgia.*
– *To remain in South Georgia for at least twelve months.*

— *To make an expenditure of about £400.*

This amount includes passages between London and Port Stanley, Assistant's salary, and complete outfit, estimating 15% [interest on capital value] *on £200 worth of scientific instruments on loan.*

Bruce was essentially a conservationist, but he recognised the necessity of commercial exploitation of natural resources in order to attract capital to exotic, far–away places. He advocated the development of a shore-base for whaling and sealing on South Georgia and also suggested the introduction of sheep, deer, cattle and even the growing of crops in the hope that this would provide safe passage for scientists in the area, and accommodation for them. He further advocated the exploitation of seals which were in abundance, and the careful control of seals which had been so blatantly overfished in the islands off the Antarctic Peninsula. In the event it was the Norwegians who developed the whaling industry off South Georgia, and who introduced reindeer to the islands.

South Georgia, a large isolated sub–Antarctic island lying around 54°S, discovered (in 1675) and then claimed for King George III by Captain James Cook in 1775, was ideally placed for sealing and whaling. Unfortunately, the Royal Geographical Society felt unable to support Bruce's scheme materially at that time.

On 6 November 1895 Bruce was working at the Ben Nevis Observatory (see chapter 3). He was probably experiencing many idle hours between taking meteorological observations and his yearnings to return to Antarctica increased. He wrote again to Mill on the possibility of leaving Scotland in September of the following year on an expedition to overwinter in Antarctica in 1897:

I count my scientific work as beginning on the day I land and ending in 12 months when I should again step on board ship. The chief work will be meteorology – hourly records, Magnetism at South Pole, and collecting specimens.

Bruce was planning an Antarctic expedition aboard two ships and his plans included Carsten Borchgrevink and the Norwegian whaler Henryk Johan Bull. Interestingly, the papers relating to this proposal throw light on apparent friction between Borchgrevink and Bull.

In January 1896 Borchgrevink wrote to Bruce, regarding Bruce's plans to overwinter in Antarctica, suggesting that the two of them collaborate. However this set of correspondence was concluded by a brief letter from Borchgrevink that ended: 'I see that you already have made arrangements with Mr H. J. Bull and regret therefore that we can not co-operate.'

The animosity between Borchgrevink and Bull seemed, at least in part, to have stemmed from Bull's belief that Borchgrevink had claimed first sighting of Victoria Land for himself without acknowledgment of Bull's role in the discovery. Bruce was later to grumble that Borchgrevink, in leading the first expedition to overwinter in Antarctica, had largely followed a plan that he himself had developed but had had to abandon the previous year. He explained the background in a postscript to a letter he wrote in February 1898 to Dr Neill of the New School of Medicine, Edinburgh.

I have always thought it strange that Borch. never made any acknowledgement that I had been trying to get the 'Antarctic's' people to land me in Victoria Land in order that I might winter there & make an attempt at reaching the magnetic pole long before he ever set sail in the 'Antarctic'. And that I had practically arranged with the owner to take me for the trip, when my plans were baulked by the vessel being disabled at the Campbell Islands .... I feel sure that he must have known about my plans, as I was in communication with Mr. Svend Foyn (owner), Mr John Bull (S. Foyn's business manager in Norway), Mr. H. J. Bull (colonial manager, Melbourne, who sailed south with the vessel) & Captain Christensen, who was in command.

[It is worth noting that Bruce's interest was in the magnetic pole, a scientific goal, not the geographical pole.]

The plan to collaborate with Bull also foundered. Bruce and Burn Murdoch had discussed a project with him to establish a whaling station at Grytviken, South Georgia, where there was a fine sheltered harbour, and to appoint Carl Anton Larsen as manager. This scheme was outlined in a meeting held in the rooms of the Royal Scottish Geographical Society in the presence of John Murray, and the commercial whalers Messrs. Currie and Salvesen; no progress was made as the whalers were unconvinced of the viability of the scheme.

Would the Royal Geographical Society offer support this time? Bruce believed that the Hon. Walter Rothschild would provide a financial advance, but the success of the expedition would depend essentially on the catching of blue whales (*Balaenoptera musculus*) and black whales (probably the humpback whale, *Magaptera novaeangliae*). 'Of course I shall have nothing to do with the commercial arrangements,' Bruce stated. 'The scientific organisation is my department.'

Keltie required more information and wondered whether Bruce was involved with the plans currently under discussion with Carsten Borchgrevink. Bruce replied on 11 March 1896, revealing that the sponsor of his expedition was Bull, who had previously led the Norwegian sealing and whaling expedition of 1893–95, and who had a vessel available worth £8350.

Of Borchgrevink, Bruce asked, 'Has he really got the funds? I am not going with him. He approached me re. cooperation and then wrote to say he would not join with me.'

In order to reassure Keltie that there was no duplication of effort, Bruce added that he had intended to go to Victoria Land, but if Borchgrevink was going there then Bruce would go 200 miles (322km) further south than Cape Adare, or alternatively he would go to the foot of Mount Erebus, McMurdo Bay.

In the event Borchgrevink, with the patronage of the publisher Sir George Newnes, led the British Antarctic Expedition of 1898-1900 aboard the *Southern Cross*. In the meantime Bruce, though not involved in either the Bull or Borchgrevink expeditions, was becoming increasingly respected as a polar naturalist of great promise and an authority worth consulting. However, he was also naturalist without employment and thus very eager to pursue new projects and new directions.

References

Bull, Henryk Johan: *The Cruise of the Atlantic* (London, 1896).

Burn Murdoch, William Gordon: *From Edinburgh to the Antarctic* (London: Longman, Green and Co, 1894) (reprinted, Bungay, 1984).

Bruce, William Speirs: 'Animal Life Observed during a Voyage to Antarctic Seas' in *Proceedings of the Royal Physical Society of Edinburgh,* vol XII; and *Journal of the Manchester Geographical Society*, vol 10 (1894).

Mill, Hugh Robert: *Life Interests of a Geographer, 1861-1944* (East Grinstead: issued privately, 1945). Available at the Scott Polar Research Institute.

Tonneson, J N and A O Johnsen: *The History of Modern Whaling* (London, 1982).

CHAPTER 3

THE BEN NEVIS INTERLUDE

THE High Level Meteorological Station on the summit of Ben Nevis was officially opened on 17 October 1883 by Mrs Colin Campbell whose property formed part of the western side of the mountain. Only one room of the observatory was finished at that time, the remainder being completed the following year. The concept of a high level station on the highest mountain in the British Isles had first been mooted by Thomas Stevenson in 1875, and endorsed in 1877 by the chairman of the council of the Scottish Meteorological Society, D Milne Home. Stevenson prepared a plan in 1879 and monies were raised from the principal scientific societies in Britain and by public subscription.

The idea of obtaining continuous recordings from a high mountain summit which could be compared with records at lower stations was immediately attractive to scientists. Ben Nevis offered all the right conditions: at 4406 feet (1343m), on the west coast of Scotland, the mountain faced the prevailing south westerlies and experienced rapidly changing meteorological conditions. Moreover, access to the foot of the mountain from Fort William was generally available all year round, and with the construction of a graded track the supply of provisions and instruments to the summit proved comparatively easy, except in extreme conditions at certain times of the year. A complementary permanent station was therefore provided and manned at the public school close to sea level in Fort William, the two stations operating as one observatory with interchangeable staff. The stations were also linked by telegraph. The summit building, made from rough-hewn dry-stone walls that were perfectly warm and dry in the bitterly cold winter months, consisted of a single storey with laboratory, telegraph office, kitchen and bedrooms, surmounted by an observatory tower made of wood for reasons of safety and to avoid any possible interference with magnetic instruments.

When Bruce returned from the Dundee Whaling Expedition he was not inclined to return to his university studies which had been interrupted for almost a full year. He wrote to Mill: 'I am burning to be off again anywhere, but particularly to the far South where I believe there is a vast sphere

Ben Nevis Observatory. (*Courtesy of the Met Office*)

for research.' Mill recalled in his autobiography that Sir Alexander Buchan, the doyen of Scottish and indeed all British meteorologists

> ... had liked to encourage all science students to practise meteorological observations, and gave them opportunities to do so as volunteer assistants in the High Level Observatory at Ben Nevis. Among those trained in this way were H N Dickson and A J Herbertson, both of whom did valuable original work in climatology, and the former served as President of the Royal Meteorological Society in 1911-1912. One of the Edinburgh students who took the Ben Nevis course was W S Bruce, who later made meteorology an essential part of his expedition in the Scotia.

In 1895 Bruce applied to work at the high level station and was supposedly appointed to replace Robert Traill Omond, a first rate meteorologist (and according to Mill, 'an original genius') who had acted as superintendent since its inception.

Not for the first time fortune appeared to smile on Bruce. The contacts he had made in his days with the Challenger laboratory, and during his university courses, were proving fruitful. He wrote to Mill on 12 September 1895:

I am seeking to train myself to be able to take charge of an Antarctic Meteorological

Observatory during one or more years, and I am glad to say that at the end of four months work, during which I have held the position of locum tenens, *Dr. Buchan has asked me whether I would become a member of the permanent staff and I have accepted the offer. I shall thus, in a miniature way be experiencing the rigours of a polar winter and trust to be more than ever fitted for the duties of an Antarctic Meteorologist and Explorer.*

[However, there appears some doubt about Bruce's official position in the observatory. He claimed to be Omond's replacement, but was appointed second assistant to Angus Rankin the new superintendent. Newly-discovered correspondence on this matter has been fully investigated by Geoffrey N Swinney in his article, 'William Speirs Bruce and the Ben Nevis Observatory' (2002).]

Omond was later to advise Bruce on the construction of the meteorological observatory on Laurie Island, South Orkneys. The observatory was built of the same kind of rough dry-stone walling as the structure on Ben Nevis and named 'Omond House' by Bruce. It remains the oldest continuously-inhabited site in Antarctica, although Omond House itself is now a ruin.

Another of Buchan's protégés was Robert Cockburn Mossman, son of an Edinburgh merchant who became one of Scotland's best meteorologists.

Mossman never attended university, and chose not to enter his father's business, but managed to persuade his father to equip a weather station for him in their large garden. Mossman occupied the low level station, while Bruce was on the summit; and through this association was asked to accompany Bruce on the Scottish National Antarctic Expedition. Mossman took control of Omond House for its first two years, thereafter becoming an important figure in the early years of the Argentine Meteorological Service.

Two other Ben Nevis observers who were to be connected with Antarctica were Angus Rankin, the first assistant to Omond on the opening of the high level station, who later took over from Mossman on Laurie Island; and David W Wilton whom Bruce met first in Franz Josef Land in 1896, and brought back with him to Edinburgh. Wilton was given a temporary position on Ben Nevis at an intermediate station which was occupied periodically, and he was eventually recruited by Bruce for the Scottish National Antarctic Expedition.

Winter conditions on Ben Nevis were generally extreme, with the observers snowed in, able to reach the outside only by snow tunnels specially constructed in order to get to the external instruments. For several months at a time the station was inaccessible by the track, but they ensured enough provisions for six months. Although winter temperatures were not excessively low (a minimum of 9.9°F [-12.3°C] had been recorded in the early days), being generally 15 to 25°F (-9.4 to -3.9°C), with a mean temperature in February of 22°F (-5.5°C), the observatory was frequently shrouded in fog and mist, strong gales were common, and ice crystals grew into pillars to windward. In effect, Bruce was experiencing the Antarctic environment he craved for. In summer the mean daily temperatures were tolerable, with 42°F (5.5°C) in July, the warmest month. Total rainfall for the year was around 146 inches (371cm).

The site was particularly good for the observation of optical phenomena including 'coronas', 'spectres' and 'glories' (strange and often very beautiful images projected from mountain summits and on ice-covered surfaces; the images appear as halos, moons and crosses, *etc*).

Bruce on skis on Ben Nevis. He was to become the first president of the Scottish Ski Club. (*Edinburgh University Library*)

Bruce was learning the discipline of regular recording of scientific information, taking his turn at the four-hour watches. The instrument array included thermometers (maximum, minimum, dry and wet bulb, radiation); rain and snow gauges; ozone tests; anemometer;

and sunshine recorder. The observatory also took the opportunity to entertain eminent visitors in the summer and it was visited by academics and politicians alike. Bruce was able to demonstrate the workings of the observatory to, among others, Hugh Robert Mill, the geologist Sir Archibald Geikie, the physicist Professor C T R Wilson, and the influential Harvard Professor of Physical Geography, William Morris Davis. Thus he forged further important links with scientists who might act as referees when raising funds for his future polar schemes, or provide advice or scientific equipment for his expeditions.

Apart from meteorology Bruce also found time for other studies, in so far as the limitations of the extreme site allowed, and he made a collection of insects which is now in the National Museums of Scotland.

However Bruce's time on the summit was destined to be cut short by Mill in London. In June 1896 Mill, in his capacity as librarian at the Royal Geographical Society, had been asked to send another naturalist to the Jackson–Harmsworth Expedition entering its third year on Franz Josef Land. He telegraphed Bruce on the summit of Ben Nevis. Could Bruce be ready to go in five days' time? Bruce required little persuasion and hurried to St Katherine's Dock in the Port of London to board *Windward*, which was taking supplies to the expedition members already out in Franz Josef Land. When it was discovered that he was without a suitable outfit for an Arctic cruise, Bruce was clothed mainly from the wardrobe of Mill, and he left the Thames on 9 June 1896 bound for his first experience of the Arctic.

Although Bruce went back briefly to Ben Nevis on his return from the Jackson–Harmsworth Expedition, his future at that time seemed uncertain and he made serious enquiries about a vacant post of curator of the Raffles Museum in Singapore. He went as far as to ask friends for references, but in the end withdrew his interest. How different might his career have been had he moved to the tropics?

Sadly the Ben Nevis Observatory was forced to close due to lack of funds in October 1904. All that remains today is a commemorative plaque.

References

Anon: *Guide to Ben Nevis, with an Account of the Foundation and Work of the Meteorological Observatory, 1893* (Edinburgh: John Menzies and Co., on behalf of the Directors of the Ben Nevis Observatory, 1893).

Mill, Hugh Robert: *The Record of the Royal Geographical Society, 1830-1930* (London: Royal Geographical Society, 1930).

Mill, Hugh Robert: *Life Interests of a Geographer, 1861-1944* (East Grinstead: issued privately, 1945). Available at the Scott Polar Research Institute.

Royal Meteorological Society: *Ben Nevis Observatory, 1883-1904* (Bracknell, 1983).

Swinney, G N: 'William Speirs Bruce, the Ben Nevis Observatory and Antarctic Meteorology' in *Scottish Geographical Journal* (2003).

CHAPTER 4

EXPLORING THE ARCTIC

Franz Josef Land (Zemlya Frantsa-Iosifa)

THE Jackson-Harmsworth Arctic Expedition left London in June 1896 bound for Franz Josef Land (now known as Zemlya Frantsa-Iosifa), an archipelago in the Arctic Ocean lying between 80° and 82°N, and today part of the Russian Federation. Although it had been discovered in 1873 by an Austro-Hungarian expedition under Karl Weyprecht and Julius Payer, little was known of its natural history and the island group was considered politically unclaimed territory. For most of the year the archipelago is ice-bound, but it can be approached by ship from the south during summer. George Frederick Jackson established his headquarters at Elmwood, Cape Flora, on the south-west of Northbrook Island.

Jackson was well known in the 1890s as a big game hunter and planned to shoot polar bears as well as other wildlife on this expedition, although its stated aims were two-fold: to carry out scientific studies throughout the three years of its Arctic encampment, and to pioneer a route to the North Pole. Accordingly appointments were made to the scientific staff. In the first year Harry Fisher was recruited as botanist; Albert Armitage, formerly a Merchant Navy officer in the P&O Line, was put in charge of meteorology, magnetic and astronomical observations; Reginald Koettlitz, a medical doctor, was appointed as geologist; and J F Child as mineralogist and photographer. This group, together with Burgess the cook, and general hands K Blomkvist, H A H Dunsford and J W Heywood, were the established residents of Elmwood. Others, like Bruce, joined them later.

The expedition was financed by Alfred Harmsworth, later Lord North-cliffe, a pioneer newspaper proprietor who founded the *Daily Mail* and *Daily Mirror* newspapers in London. This was the era of universal education, and of the popular press, at least in the western world, and this kind of sponsored journalistic enterprise originated in America where the notorious owner/editor of the *New York Herald*, James Gordon Bennett, sought exclusive rights to publish the accounts of exotic travellers and their expeditions. By commissioning an expedition, the newspaper obtained exclusive rights to copy, and tales of exploration helped to sell newspapers. Notable accounts included Henry Morton Stanley's East African search for David Livingstone,

Lieutenant Frederick Schwatka's Arctic expedition (1878), and the disastrous Arctic drift of George Washington de Long's *Jeanette* (1879-81).

Alfred Harmsworth's London rival, Sir George Newnes, the publisher of popular magazines and self-educators, imitated Harmsworth by subsidising the British National Antarctic Expedition led by Carsten Borchgrevink in 1898-1900.

As part of the Jackson-Harmsworth Expedition, Bruce keenly anticipated the opportunities for extensive investigations into the natural history of Franz Josef Land without the frustrations and lack of co-operation encountered on the Dundee Whaling Expedition.

On the northbound journey aboard *Windward*, Bruce busied himself with meteorological measurements, sea temperatures and bird sightings, and threw sealed bottles with messages overboard to indicate ocean current flow, on the off-chance they would be recovered and reported by some other vessel or beach comber.

Windward called first at Archangel in northern Russia where a young Englishman, David W Wilton, joined the company as assistant zoologist. He had lived in Russia for many years and gained a wide experience of Arctic Russia. Consequently he was an expert in skiing and sledge-driving. On 29 June, Bruce wrote to his benefactor from the northern coast of Norway, before *Windward* shaped a course northwards for the Franz Josef islands.

S.Y. Windward, Vardo, 29.6.96

My Dear Dr. Mill

    At present we are due to take our departure from here at 8 a.m. The voyage is pleasant, but I shall be glad to leave here for the ice.

    The skipper, Captain James Brown sailed as 1st mate on board the Diana *on her Antarctic cruise. He was then qualified master and has long experience of the ice in Davis Strait, Lancaster Sound, etc. Greenland Sea and Kara Sea. He has been very friendly so far and I hope that he will turn out alright. The first mate is also a good fellow, and he and the second have both been whalers. These last three are Peterhead men. The rest of the crew are of all nations. The cook and the steward are the only two Englishmen. Wilton my companion is a young English fellow, 23 years, who has lived in Russia a long time and is experienced with ski and sleigh and I think we shall get on first rate.*

    Yesterday, Sunday was spent in gathering Vardo plants, and I got many species, but the flora has to be worked up and I don't expect anything new. I have to thank Mrs. Mill and yourself for your kind hospitality and for the interest you have taken in my departure. I am eager for work and I shall especially value being in the northern ice. I hope however to be sailing once more for the south after the return next autumn.

[Of those with whom Bruce was destined to spend the next year, three would visit the Antarctic within the next few years: Armitage and Koettlitz joined Captain Scott's Discovery Expedition in 1901-04, and Wilton, as mentioned earlier, was recruited by Bruce for the Scotia Expedition.]

Ice was first sighted in 76°N on 6 July, over 200 miles from Franz Josef Land, and the ship made slow progress thereafter before arriving off Cape Flora three weeks later. Here at Elmwood, to the complete astonishment of everyone aboard *Windward*, they found Fridtjof Nansen and his companion, Hjalmar Johansen. Both had been given up for lost many months before.

Nansen, in his ship *Fram,* had left Norway in 1893 in an attempt to reach the North Pole by allowing his ship to be frozen into the ice and carried northwards by the Arctic currents. It had become clear by March 1895 that the ship would not cross the Pole and Nansen and Johansen had set out on foot across the ice. Having reached 86°N, they turned south in order to reach either Spitsbergen or Franz Josef Land. Their companions were left behind, imprisoned in the helpless *Fram*. Forced to winter in a small hut crudely built of stones and walrus hide, Nansen and Johansen had restarted their southerly journey in the spring of 1896 and on 17 June were spotted by Armitage four miles (6.4km) away from Cape Flora. Jackson fired his gun in the air to attract the two men and hurried to meet them, supposing them to be Russian or Norwegian trappers. The encounter has become one of the most historic of all polar exploration:

Aren't you Nansen?
Yes, I'm Nansen.
Well, I'm damned glad to see you.

Nansen and Johansen recuperated at Elmwood and sailed back to Norway in *Windward* on 7 August. Meanwhile, unknown to those at Elmwood, at the time Nansen and Johansen were discovered in Franz Josef Land the *Fram* broke free from the ice to the north of Spitsbergen. All who had remained on board were safe, and when *Windward* reached Tromsø, Nansen and Johansen were reunited with their companions.

For Bruce the fortuitous meeting with Nansen meant yet one more influential polar explorer and celebrity who would give unstinting advice and friendship over the years. They were to meet up again later both in Edinburgh and Spitsbergen.

Bruce recounted his early days at Cape Flora in a letter to Mill dated 30 July 1896:

… We arrived here on the 26th nearly three weeks in the ice. I am asking Mr. Harmsworth to send me out two reversing thermometers and two deep-sea water

bottles among other things. Any practical hints you can give me as to the use of the water bottle I shall be glad of as I have not used it before. Also any further suggestions as to further work. I have sounded, taken surface temperatures, salinities, thrown out floats [bottles], and noted colour of sea besides taking 4 hourly meteorological observations, and Mr. Wilton, my companion, has given me assistance in making these the more complete. It is most unfortunate that both of us have been maimed, Wilton with a very bad finger disabling his right hand shortly after leaving Vardo and I my left knee by falling down the after hatch shortly after leaving London. Neither of us have recovered yet but within a week we hope to be all right again.

I should be very much obliged if when the vessel comes out again you will give me a summary of Antarctic news as my future movements will depend a good deal upon the news. I am on for further developing and carrying out plans for further work in the south. I have talked with Nansen and hope to have the opportunity for another talk. I believe in him so thoroughly. Who could help doing so?

Please give my kindest regards to Mrs. Mill — the same yourself.

There was much to do at Cape Flora for Bruce and Wilton, although Bruce found himself, as on the Dundee Whaling Expedition, expected to make time to prepare skins as well as prepare his own specimens. This time it was bears shot by Jackson. His zoological collection consisted of marine specimens as well as terrestrial and he later sent a comparative account of his collection to Mill to demonstrate the extent of his work:

Zoological Collections of North Polar Expeditions

German East Greenland	(1869-70)	Naturalists 3	Years 1	Species 316
British North Polar	(1875-76)	2	1	294
United States International	(1881-83)	2	2	295
Austro-Hungarian North Polar	(1872-74)	2	2	139
Jackson-Harmsworth	(1896-99)	1	1	611

Such expeditions as Greeley's (1882-84), and others did practically no zoological work. I think I will be able to bring my list up to at least 700 species; there ought to have been more but I had only 8 hours to get everything ready in. I had to make tow-nets out of my pocket handkerchiefs, rope out of loose spun yarn, and everything was on the same makeshift scale.

In spite of his hurried departure from London on *Windward* and the consequent shortage of specialised collecting instruments, Bruce brought back an extensive collection of skins, eggs and skeletons which were eventually kept for many years in his Scottish Oceanographical Laboratory in Nicolson Street, Edinburgh. He had been obliged to improvise. Having no coverslips with him, he made 100 substitutes by cutting microscope slides into four parts. In an appendix to an account of the expedition given by Jackson to the Royal Geographical Society in London (*Geographical Journal*, 1898), Bruce commented on his collection which was mainly marine from depths down to 234 fathoms, mostly from depths between 18 and 26 fathoms. He had large numbers of invertebrates, and three species of birds hitherto unreported in that area. Of mammals, only the polar bear and arctic fox were represented. He published a paper with the great ornithologist, William Eagle Clark, *Mammalia and Birds of Franz Josef Land* (Royal Physical Society of Edinburgh); and, also with Eagle Clark, an article on the Franz Josef birds in *Ibis* for April 1898.

Although others on the *Windward* regarded themselves as part of a hunting expedition, Bruce did not possess a gun and was against the shooting of wildlife except for food, self-protection or in the name of scientific research. Jackson, on the other hand, shot over 100 polar bears during his three-year stay, all meticulously recorded in the Game Book, as well as walrus, seals, foxes and birds of all kinds. There was no shortage of fresh meat for the occupants of Elmwood, with delicious bear steaks and the breasts of birds, especially guillemot or loon, almost always available. On one notable day, 16 August 1896, Jackson shot 146 loons destined for the pot. Such was his expertise, that the next day he killed 92 out of 100 consecutively in flight.

Some specimens, however, were shot for further research, and in Jackson's popular account of the expedition, *A Thousand Days in the Arctic* (London, 1899), he indicates some disagreement with Bruce:

> *Specimens prepared by Dr Koettlitz were sent to the British Museum for examination, and it is a matter of some regret that those that Mr. Bruce had in his possession were not despatched there also, so that the collection could have been treated as a whole, or on the other hand, Mr. Harmsworth and myself would gladly have consented to the remainder of the specimens being submitted to Mr. Eagle Clarke, who it must be confessed has done his description of the portion of the collection entrusted to him in his usual admirable and complete manner.*

Bruce appears to have been guilty here of a lack of tact and a tendency towards scientific conceit, flaws in his character that would be held against him in later life.

Although references to Bruce are few in Jackson's book, he mentions him in a more positive light in his article for the *Geographical Journal*:

> *Bruce was our zoologist, a work in which in this part of the world it is frequently carried on under circumstances the reverse of agreeable. It is no pleasant job to dabble in icy-cold water, with the thermometer some degrees below zero, or to plod in the*

summer through snow, slush, and mud many miles in search of animal life, as I have known Mr. Bruce frequently to do.

Jackson also memorialised the young man by naming Cape Bruce after him in the north of the island at 80°55N.

In spite of the original aims, the Jackson–Harmsworth Expedition made no serious attempt to pioneer a route to the Pole. It had become primarily a hunting trip, although the scientific results were by no means negligible. Koettlitz, for example, helped to demonstrate the dietary importance of fresh meat, for all those at Elmwood remained in excellent health throughout their stay; whilst the crew of *Windward*, who had been frozen in the ice during the winter of 1894–95 (before Bruce joined), existed on tinned foodstuffs and showed signs of incipient scurvy.

In part-defence of his failure to make an attempt on the Pole, Jackson reprinted in his book a letter published by Alfred Harmsworth in the public press in 1894, before the expedition left London:

As to Mr. Jackson's chances of reaching the Pole I shall say nothing. For my own part, I shall be entirely satisfied if he and his companions add to our knowledge of the geography and flora and fauna of Franz Josef Land and the area lying immediately north of it. With 'beating the record' north I have very little sympathy. If Mr. Jackson plants the Union Flag nearer the Pole than the Stars and Stripes (who head us by four miles only), I shall be glad, but if he came back, having found the Pole, but minus the work of the scientists, of which our expedition consists, I should regard the venture as a failure.

During 1897 Franz Josef Land was visited by *Balaena*, Bruce's ship from the Dundee Expedition. Its captain was Thomas Robertson whom Bruce had previously met as captain of *Active* in the same expedition. The renewal of their acquaintance led directly to the recruitment in 1902 of Robertson as master of *Scotia* for the Scottish National Antarctic Expedition.

The Jackson–Harmsworth Expedition finally left Elmwood in July 1897 and reached the Thames on 3 September. On the return journey Bruce saw a tantalising glimpse of Bear Island, the southernmost island of the Spitsbergen archipelago, an island group that was to occupy him for many years later in his life.

Novaya Zemlya

After the Jackson-Harmsworth Expedition, Bruce went back to Edinburgh accompanied by David Wilton who registered for a degree in natural science at the university. Bruce was without regular employment once again and had no private income, but he worked for a short time as assistant to John Arthur Thomson and continued his work at the Ben Nevis station for a few months. In 1898, however, Bruce was offered the opportunity to return to the Arctic to join Major Andrew Coats in his steam yacht *Blencathra* on a hunting and pleasure cruise to Spitsbergen and the waters off Novaya Zemlya. The original invitation had been intended for Hugh Robert Mill, but Clements Markham, as president of the Royal Geographical Society, had refused the Society's librarian leave and Mill generously offered his place to Bruce.

Andrew Coats wrote to Mill on 3 March 1898 from Quenby Hall, Leicester:

I have your note this morning which was sent up to me here where I am staying at present. I am to be in London tomorrow, Friday 4, and I will call on you at your office and have a talk. I think Mr. Bruce would be a most valuable acquisition. I should like to understand exactly from you if he would accept a salary for his services, say in taking notes and writing down a log of the trip etc. or whether he would wish to be on his own hook entirely. It is easier for me to get this from you than to ask him directly. In the first case I should require to get some instruments and perhaps you could give me an idea when I call tomorrow what would be required. Don't trouble to answer. I shall call about 2.30 at your office and hope to see you.

Andrew Coats was the cousin of Andrew Coates [*sic*] of Perth whom Bruce had met on the quayside at Dundee in 1892 and who had given Bruce five pounds to equip himself for the Antarctic whaling expedition. The owner of *Blencathra* was a member of the wealthy family of textile manufactures of Paisley and the family were later instrumental in financing Bruce's Scotia Expedition. *Blencathra* was a sportsman's steam yacht, luxuriously equipped for pleasure cruising.

Bruce, travelling as naturalist, had to equip himself with essential scientific instruments. He turned once more to Mill who lent him one deep-sea water bottle and one deep-sea thermometer from the Royal Geographical Society's stores on 21 April 1898. Confident about the contribution he could now make to an Arctic expedition, Bruce had written to Mill on 27 March 1898:

My Dear Dr. Mill
I have to thank you most sincerely for having mentioned my name to Coats and I hope you will not think me too ungrateful for not doing so before as I have been

in bed with influenza. I was not well at Leicester and had to take to bed at once on my return. I was only up on Thursday and on Friday I was out for the first time having to lecture that night, which I am glad to say I was none the worse yesterday beyond feeling rather jagged.

Coats has arranged to take me on for £15 a month and to give me a liberal outfit; wants me to see about the scientific instruments. I shall be very glad of any private hints you can give me although I understand from Mr. Coats that you are not able to give hints from your official position. I have a fairly good idea I think of what is needed but you are sure to think of some things I might overlook. I am going round to see the Blencathra soon as she comes into the Clyde.

I have tried to emphasise to Coats the importance of certain topographical work in Franz Josef Land district. To determine whether there are or not any islands between Cape Mary Harmsworth and White Island (Nansen still thinks there may be). To determine more definitely the existence or non-existence of King Oscar Land and if possible Peterman Land (Jackson doesn't put in King Oscar Land). The east coast of Wichet Land I am afraid is too big an order. But there is any amount of sounding, dredging, trawling in the sounds and fiords to be done and physical works, currents, salinities, etc. If we have an open sea like last year there. If you think it worth while pushing any of these points to Coats it might come better from you than too emphatically from me as I don't wish to assume the position of 'boss'. I have just mentioned them to him and he seems inclined to try Franz Josef Land. I told him I didn't care and didn't feel able to undertake medical work. I mentioned a Dr. T N Johnston who has been helping me with my Franz Josef Land collections and who is very keen to go without salary and would be a great help to me. I wish he had thought of taking him but I think he is taking a retired army surgeon.

There is no reason why we should not do this easily. Of course I recognise that the conditions may be reversed this year. But I don't think there should be difficulty in getting to Franz Josef Land and as there seems to be a possibility of Andrée being at Cape Flora I think we should.

Arthur Thomson is giving Wilton a little for the summer session in return for helping him in the laboratory and in demonstrating and Turnbull will give him his class out in return for an hour's help a day so that he will just be able to pull through a summer session and likely pass in botany zoology at the end of it. At the beginning of next week (tomorrow and Wednesday) he finishes his Prelim. And will I think get through unless they plough him in Russian!! On Friday he goes to Ben Nevis for the vacation. After the summer session he has no funds at all, so that if you happen to hear of any work that would suit him especially I think if it would enable him to remain in Edinburgh and finish his First Professional in Medicine, I am sure he would be most indebted to you.

With kind regards to Mrs. Mill and yourself,
Wm S Bruce

Andrew Coats' hunting party aboard *Blencathra*. (Royal Scottish Geographical Society [RSGS])

Blencathra left the Clyde on 1 May 1898 bound for the Arctic, but Bruce waited behind for delivery of the new Lucas sounding machine with two coils of wire allowing sounding to depths of 2500 fathoms. He then travelled on the mail steamer from Newcastle to Bergen and followed the coast north, calling at 44 settlements on the way to catch up with *Blencathra* in Tromsø. The ship then sailed north for the Barents Sea, Novaya Zemlya and Kolguev, before returning to Vardo for re-victualling. From there, in July 1898, he wrote to Mill about the cruise:

> *My Dear Dr. Mill*
>
> *Yours is the only letter I have received so I cannot leave you without one in return. Wellman was here for a few hours the day before yesterday and has gone on to Archangel for 84 dogs and a house. You likely know his plans for wintering in N. Franz Josef Land and pushing north. He and his three American companions and the Norwegian captain of the 'Fridtjof' came on board.*
>
> *I have been taking 4 hourly observations in meteorology and temperature of the sea surface; have collected samples of sea water from surface and a few from below, have tested salinity with Buchanan's hydrometer; my tow-nets fine of course have been going almost constantly and I have had a few hauls of the trawl north of Kolguev and off N. Zemlya. Soundings also and temperatures below sea surface.*
>
> *This is a pure yachting cruise and life is luxurious, still I hope to get some decent results. But how I long to have a more purely scientific trip. I think it might be worth*

Prince of Monaco, scientists, officers and crew aboard *Princesse Alice* (Bruce, extreme right). *(RSGS)*

my while to try and raise friends to charter, or buy and then sell again, a good walrus sloop for a summer's work along the ice edge. Such a boat could be bought for six or eight hundred pounds.

I have just heard of Murray's honour, it is not conferred on him too soon. Thanks for your letter and the views of the German Expedition which I had not heard of. I mentioned it to Coats, to whom as well as to Cockburn and Reid I have given your message. They wish me to return the compliment.

Please give my kindest regards to Mrs. Mill,
accept same yourself, from,
Yours very sincerely
Wm S Bruce

We have no very definite plans but go where the ice is sufficiently open. Perhaps the east coast of Spitsbergen will be our first attempt, and if open, F J Land and north-wards, but the Blencathra *is not the ship the* Balaena *is as far as ice is concerned and I don't think she is as strong even as the* Windward. *Caution therefore is necessary.*

The cruise, as predicted by Bruce, did shape a course for the Spitsbergen archipelago, but finding access to Spitsbergen blocked by ice that, despite the summer, had not yet retreated north, they returned to Tromsø in July. To Bruce's surprise and delight they found *Princesse Alice*, the ship built for

Prince Albert of Monaco in 1898 for oceanographic work, berthed in the harbour there. It was the finest equipped scientific vessel since *Challenger*. *Blencathra's* personnel were welcomed aboard *Princesse Alice* and entertained by the Prince. When the Prince invited Bruce to accompany him on a hydrographic survey to Spitsbergen, Bruce found himself once more heading for Arctic waters instead of returning to Scotland. Before sailing, he hurriedly wrote to Mill to inform him of his unexpected change of plans:

Tromsø, Norway, 27.7.98

My Dear Dr. Mill

A pleasant voyage on the Blencathra *is at an end and I return to Spitsbergen neighbourhood as the Prince of Monaco's guest on board* Princesse Alice. *I am in great haste and have only time to tell you this much and to thank you most sincerely for having enabled me to go once more, I may even say twice more to the north. In our last cruise we circumnavigated Bear Island, attempted landing on Hope Island, saw King Charles Islands, and Edge Island. Did some trawling and dredging, townetting, when possible. Shot birds, bears, seals, walrus. Took physical observations. You know what real revelling there will be in zoological and physical work. J Y Buchanan and Prof. Brandt of Kiel are also guests. But I have no time as we are off. I have been very busy getting on board. I will tell you afterwards about it.*

Bruce was continuing his apprenticeship as a polar oceanographer. On the Coats expedition he listed the scientific work completed:

34 *hawls with dredge trawl and trap*
60 *gatherings of surface plankton*
88 *soundings, 57 being in new locations*
30 *salinity observations*
147 *floats thrown out at 37 stations.*

Aboard *Princesse Alice* Bruce was now in the company of some of the best oceanographers in Europe. Dr Jules Richard, a French biologist, was in charge of the Prince's scientific party; the Scottish chemist John Young Buchanan was known to Bruce from the Challenger office in Edinburgh; and Professor Karl Brandt was a physical oceanographer. The vessel was in the charge of Captain Henry Charlwood Carr, the Prince's regular commander.

This time the scientists were able to land on Bear Island and Bruce climbed Mount Misery to view the interior and collect birds and plants before the ship sailed to the west coast of the principal island of the archipelago. They visited the large Stor Fiord (Storfjord), Sassen Bay (Sassenfjorden), Advent Bay (Adventfjorden) and Klaas Billen Bay, before steaming north to the former sealer's harbour of Smeerenburg Sound. At Dane's Island they viewed the remains of the luckless Saloman August Andrée's balloon house (he tragically disappeared in a balloon in his search for the North Pole), before ultimately reaching latitude 84°34N. As Brandt and Buchanan had left the expedition earlier in Advent Bay, Bruce was placed in charge of the observations.

Once the expedition was over Bruce returned to Edinburgh, but only briefly. The Prince of Monaco invited him to spend the winter in Monte Carlo and continue his oceanographic work on *Princesse Alice* in the Mediterranean. Bruce would then return to Spitsbergen with the Prince in 1899 for detailed hydrographic surveying throughout the summer. (It was on these voyages that Bruce noted the long island of Prince Charles Foreland [Prins Karls Forland] and he was to return in 1906 with Prince Albert to make the first systematic survey and map of the island.)

On the voyage north to Spitsbergen in 1899, *Princesse Alice* first called at Kiel where the Kaiser was reviewing the German Fleet. Bruce shared in the general celebrations and later visited the Empress Eugenie in her yacht *Thistle*, cruising with her along the Norwegian Lyngen Fiord. *Princesse Alice* then steamed north to Spitsbergen and along the west coast, eventually reaching Red Bay (80°N). The Prince decided to spend the summer season here. It was recorded that Bruce climbed the highest nearby peak in the area, which was named 'Ben Nevis' by the Prince in his honour.

The ship sailed south to Advent Bay in the deep, sheltered Isfjord, 150 miles (241km) to the south east, returning to Red Bay in August, cautiously entering the bay. In spite of continuous soundings in apparently ten fathoms, *Princesse Alice* unexpectedly foundered on a rock and, despite strenuous attempts, could not be released under her own power. The Prince ordered the ship's small steam launch to take the only two women on board, the storekeeper's wife and another lady, back to Advent Bay and placed the off-loading of stores and camping in charge of Bruce. The company prepared themselves for possible over-wintering on the shore of Red Bay. Fortunately the ship was eventually re-floated and a rescue ship, the Swedish gunboat *Svenskund*, accompanied *Princesse Alice* back to Truerenberg where some coals were transferred before the ship sailed for a full inspection at Advent Bay. The journey continued to Tromsø where temporary repairs to the leaks could be made before *Princesse Alice* left for a major overhaul at Le Havre.

This had been a real adventure for Bruce. He had been given the opportunity to carry out work to a high professional degree as a scientist on a superbly-equipped oceanographical survey ship and had been made responsible for the safety of others at a shore camp in high northern latitudes. But his apprenticeship as polar naturalist and explorer was coming to an end. He now began to look for greater responsibility and command.

References

Bruce, William Speirs: 'With the Yachts *Blencathra* and *Princesse Alice* to the Barents and
    Greenland Seas' in *Scottish Geographical Magazine* (1899), vol 15.
Bruce, William Speirs and W Eagle Clark: 'Mammalia and Birds of Franz Josef Land' in
    Proceedings of the Royal Physical Society of Edinburgh, vol XIV, pp 78-112.
Jackson, Frederick: *A Thousand Days in the Arctic* (London: Harper and Brothers, 1899), in two
    volumes.
Jackson, Frederick: 'Three Years Exploration in Franz Josef Land' in *Geographical Journal*
    (1898), vol XI, 2.
Speak, Peter: 'Bruce and the Arctic' in the *Scottish Naturalist*, 111: 197-206.

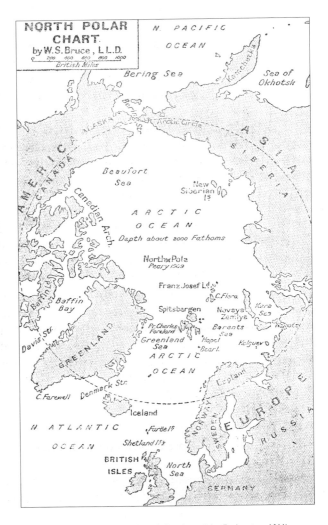

Bruce's own North Polar chart (taken from *Polar Exploration*, 1911).

CHAPTER 5

FAMILY LIFE

BRUCE could never have been described as gregarious. He had the detachment of a leader who could plan well ahead and take command, but he rarely encouraged any intimate friendship. Indeed his natural reserve was such that in correspondence he exhibited a manner that extended beyond the bounds of normal Edwardian formality. Bruce even referred to his wife as 'Mrs Bruce'.

Even those who had known and worked closely with him for years were reluctant to address him familiarly in the written word. Rudmose Brown never ventured beyond 'My Dear Bruce' in their extensive correspondence; and Bruce in turn would reply 'Dear Brown', or occasionally 'My Dear Brown'. Hugh Robert Mill and his wife were characteristically addressed as 'Dr and Mrs Mill'.

The only person who seemed to have broken his rather formal etiquette was James Ferrier, an Edinburgh solicitor and secretary to the Scotia Expedition, who addressed his letters to Bruce 'My Dear Willie', and in reply received the salutation 'My Dear Jim'.

Bruce's closest colleague after 1900, and the person who knew him best, was Rudmose Brown, who accompanied Bruce on the Scotia Expedition and shared several visits to Spitsbergen on behalf of the Scottish Spitsbergen Syndicate. No one was better qualified to write Bruce's biography after his death in 1921, and until relatively recently *A Naturalist at the Poles* has been the principal source of details on Bruce's life and career. However, for the earlier period of Bruce's life, even Rudmose Brown had to defer to Burn Murdoch for details.

John Arthur Thomson, considered a family friend, commented on Bruce's character when reviewing Rudmose Brown's book in 1924:

[He was] *a man who had more than a little of the stuff that heroes are made of, a man who did great things with a quiet will and a gentle heart, who rarely got that public recognition which was the due of his achievements.*

We knew him intimately for thirty-five years, often in very bad weather, so to speak, and we never heard him once grumble about himself, though he was neither to hold nor bend when he thought some injustice was being done to, or slight cast on, his men, on his colleagues, on his laboratory, on his Scotland. Then one got glimpses of the volcano which his gentle spirit usually kept sleeping.

In 1901, the year before the Scotia Expedition, Bruce married Jessie Mackenzie, daughter of Alexander Mackenzie of Tain, Easter Ross, on the north-east coast of Scotland. Like several of Bruce's sisters, Jessie trained as a nurse in London and she met her future husband while working for his father in his medical practice. According to their daughter, Sheila, her mother was of striking appearance with fine auburn hair. She was the youngest of a Highland family of twelve children and had ten brothers.

Bruce and Jessie had arranged to get married in the Scottish Highlands, but even for such a special event the approach of the groom was somewhat diffident, as this letter to the Mills on 23 January 1901 suggests:

My Dear Dr Mill

I was intending to tell Mrs Mill and yourself the other day that I was intending to marry, but when the time came it seemed even more difficult to say so than to reach the South Pole. Such is the case however and I should not like the event to take place without having told you since you have done so much for me ....

Mill was not the only colleague with whom Bruce was shy concerning his impending marriage, as John Young Buchanan pointed out from the Conservative Club, St James's Street, London, on 22 January 1901:

My Dear Bruce

I am afraid you must have thought me 'peu sympathetique', when you told me of your approaching marriage, but I was rather taken aback especially at the intrepidity of the proceeding. However intrepidity is just what we want in the leader of our antarctic expedition [Scotia] and now I think there can be no doubt that we have got it. I wish you and your future wife all happiness and I enclose a little wedding present which may be useful ....

The Bruces set up home in Joppa, on the southern shore of the Firth of Forth, south east of Edinburgh. Joppa was really a suburb of Portobello and was, it appeared, well known to Bruce. Correspondence during his time there came from various addresses: Newton Cottage, South Morton Street, the home of R Turnbull, in 1898; 11 Mount Pleasant in 1899; 2 Milton Road in 1902; South Morton Street in 1906-19; and finally 17 Joppa Road. The house in South Morton Street was appropriately named 'Antarctica' in 1907 (previously 'Cairnbank') and the name was transferred to 17 Joppa Road.

Joppa itself was located close to a branchline to Edinburgh and thus highly convenient for Bruce's daily journeys to the city.

Bruce and Jessie's first child was born in April 1902 (seven months before the Scotia Expedition) and named Eillium Alastair. Eillium is the Scottish Gaelic equivalent of 'William'. At first the marriage was a happy one, with accounts of holidays in the Trossachs and the Highlands; but Bruce's frequent meetings in London, his absence for over two years on the Scotia Expedition, and his summer field work from 1906 onwards in Spitsbergen, put considerable strain on the relationship. Nonetheless, their daughter, Sheila Mackenzie, was born in 1909.

Among those who gained some insight into the Bruce family life were John Arthur Thomson, Mill and his wife, and Rudmose Brown. Rudmose Brown was known affectionately to the children as 'Uncle Ginger'. In a letter sent to him at the University of Sheffield, 3 March 1910, Bruce wrote:

I have been unable to write before because in addition to the heavy work I have in hand at present Eillium after being ill on Saturday and Sunday develops full fledged measles on Monday with high temperatures up to 105F. Today he is better but it has meant for me at least sleepless nights. Mrs Bruce too has had severe neuritis in the neck, arms, and shoulders. Sheila is well so far but can scarcely avoid taking the measles too and it will be a tough business if she does, especially for herself.

Bruce wrote again to Rudmose Brown on 6 March:

Eillium is improving, the fever is gone now and he was up a little yesterday, the extra work has not improved Mrs. Bruce's neuritis however.

With no one to help around the house, and an unreliable income (Bruce remained dependent on patronage for virtually all his activities), it was clear that life as the wife of a polar naturalist and explorer was becoming more and more unattractive to Mrs Bruce. Occasionally wealthier friends, like Buchanan, would include in a letter to Bruce a treasury note with the instruction: 'The enclosed is for Mrs. Bruce to help with the housekeeping.' Nonetheless, domestic life was never easy in the Joppa household.

Bruce and Jessie became estranged around 1915 or 1916 but continued to cohabit. After Bruce's death in 1921 Jessie emigrated to Australia, married a judge, and lived there until her death in 1942.

However, despite this picture of a rather unbending, distant and private man, Bruce was remembered by his children with great affection. His daughter, Sheila, recollected him as a very loving and lovable father.

Sheila Mackenzie Bruce was twelve when her father died. She was placed in the care of her aunt Violet who sent her to a girls' boarding school in

Bruce, Eillium Alistair and Jessie. (*SPRI*)

Hertfordshire, near Bishop's Stortford. Sheila, however, tried to run away from the disciplined regime and was despatched to a finishing school for young ladies in Switzerland. Later she took up secretarial work in London. Sheila married Bill Willman, a South African, and they lived for many years near Cape Town by the ocean, where the house faced in the direction of *Scotia's* exploits at the beginning of the century. After World War II, Sheila Bruce-Willman, her husband and an adopted son, returned to England. When her husband died she moved to Bebington on the Wirral Peninsula, Merseyside until her own death in the mid-1990s.

In his will Bruce entrusted his estate to a number of Trustees – comprising his friends, Thomas B Whitson, William Gordon Burn Murdoch, Leslie Usher, Alfred N Aitken, and his sister, Violet – who were to administer the estate on behalf of his children until they turned 21, when they would become the Trustees. In this way he avoided leaving his effects solely in the hands of his wife. His estate was valued at a not inconsiderable sum of £7000 (£140,000 at today's value) for one who had such irregular sources of income, although he had few substantial items to leave. His 'Upright Grand Piano' was left to his daughter. Apparently 'Mrs Bruce' sold it immediately to a policeman living nearby in Joppa.

When Eillium was 14 his father entered him for training as a cadet on the *Worcester* moored in the Thames. Bruce wrote to the Mills, asking if they would meet his son and introduce him to the ship. Eillium prospered as a

Camping in the Scottish Highlands: (left to right) Bruce with Sheila Mackenzie, Jessie and Eillium Alastair. (*SPRI*)

Merchant Navy officer and was awarded the Order of the British Empire for services during World War II as Commander in the Royal Navy Volunteer Reserve. He completed his career as Captain of a Fisheries Research Ship, a converted mine-sweeper, the *Fluellen*. It was renamed, quite fortuitously, *Scotia*, when he took command in 1948. The ship was the first of a succession of *Scotia* research vessels. The latest, handsome in appearance and extremely well equipped, was launched by Her Majesty the late Queen Mother in 1998.

Eillium married Annie Cassidy who was from a large Irish family. Their daughter, Moira, now Moira Watson, emigrated to Hamilton, Ontario, Canada in 1967. She had seven children, Bruce's great-grandchildren. Moira trained as a teacher at Craiglockhart Training College, Edinburgh and is now retired. Her brother, William Noble Bruce, also lives in Canada, in Don Mills, near Toronto. Eillium himself died in 1969.

References

Rudmose Brown, Robert Neal: *A Naturalist at the Poles* (London, 1923).

CHAPTER 6

PREPARATIONS FOR A
SCOTTISH EXPEDITION

DURING the second half of the nineteenth century the revival of scientific interest in Antarctica experienced a slow gestation. The professional societies had always had a latent interest in high latitudes in order to increase knowledge of the natural history of the world as a whole, both in the oceans as well as on the land. However, the study of the Earth's magnetism, so vital in navigation, was still incomplete without a precise location for the south magnetic pole, and navigation in the Southern Ocean had more than a little uncertainty about it.

The British Admiralty still regarded itself as the prime mover in the exploration and charting of the coastlines of the world and there was, in the hey-day of the British Empire, a powerful belief that the Royal Navy had both the duty as well as the resources and expertise to carry out such work. Other voices were similarly raised to call forth an international expedition for the investigation of polar science, although no group advocated that the achievement of the Pole itself, without scientific investigation, should have priority, despite the fact that some individuals might well have had an unexpressed desire to claim national sovereignty over parts of newly-discovered territory.

Among the principal bodies that showed interest from time to time were the Royal Societies of London and Edinburgh, British Association for the Advancement of Science, Royal Geographical Society and Royal Scottish Geographical Society, the International Geographical Union, the newly-formed Geographical Societies of Australia, the British Admiralty, the admiralties of other countries, and various associated individuals around the world.

The call for the resumption of Antarctic exploration came in 1885 with the creation of an Antarctic committee by the British Association for the Advancement of Science. This body had been founded in 1831, a year after the creation of the Royal Geographical Society, and had as one of its prime aims the popularisation of science. To this end it promoted an annual conference held in different cities throughout the United Kingdom. Membership was

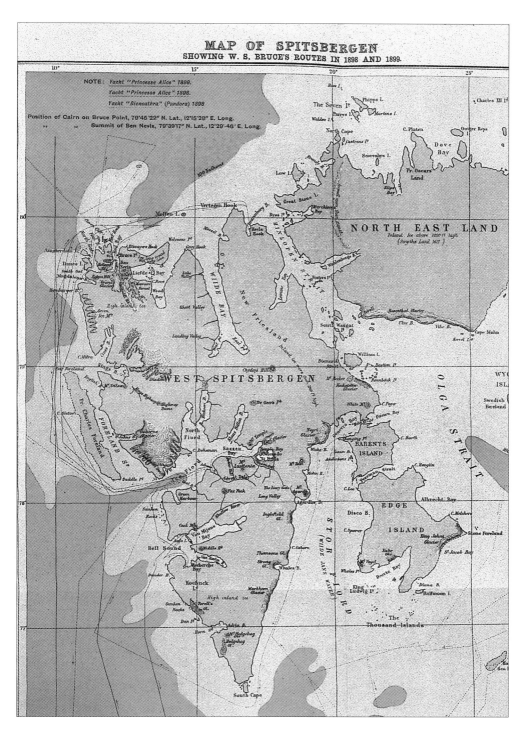

Map of Spitsbergen showing Bruce's routes in 1898 and 1899 aboard *Princesse Alice* and *Blencathra*.
(*Scottish Geographical Magazine*, 1900)

Scientists, officers and crew on board *Scotia*, with Bruce (middle, second row); piper, Gilbert Kerr (middle, front). (*EUL*)

Afternoon relaxation, Weddell Sea. (*SPRI*)

The three cooks of the *Scotia*. (*SPRI*)

Practising the pipes aboard *Scotia*. (*Royal Scottish Geographical Society* [*RSGS*])

Bruce's cabin aboard *Scotia*. (*SPRI*)

Scotia off Coats Land, flying the Union Jack and Saltire. (*SPRI*)

Scottish and Argentine staff, Laurie Island Metereological Station.
(Left to right) Martin, Harvey Pirie, Ross, Cuthbertson, Mossman, Smith (cook), Acuna, Szmula, Valette. (SPRI)

Safe anchorage in Scotia bay with temporary metereological station. (RSGS)

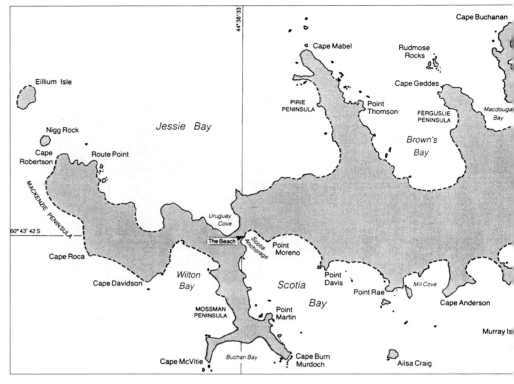

ABSTRACT OF ACCOUNT CHARGE AND DISCHARGE

Of the Intromissions of Messrs WHITSON & METHUEN, C.A., with the Funds of

The Scottish National Antarctic Expedition, 1902,

For the period from 15th January 1902 to 31st August 1905.

Receipts			£35,587 7 11
Payments—			
1. Ship		£16,730 12 10	
2. Equipment		1,751 14 0	
3. Miscellaneous		610 4 6	
4. Insurance		220 17 2	
5. Scientific Instruments		2,309 3 7	
6. Food		2,225 10 8	
Add—Subscriptions in kind from very many Scottish firms and individuals.			
7. Salaries to Scientific Staff		3,242 19 2	
8. Wages to Officers and Crew		4,823 11 7	
9. Office Expenses—			
a. Organising	£420 8 0		
b. Advertising	41 7 3		
c. Secretary's Salary, Clerk's Salary, Rent, Rates, and Taxes	1,190 14 4		
d. Outlays on Specimens	62 15 8		
		1,715 5 3	
10. Port and Voyage Expenses		1,730 19 6	
11. Management and Miscellaneous		1,044 16 8	
			36,405 14 11
Balance due to Messrs Whitson & Methuen			£818 7 0

Mr James Coats' Subscription amounted to £23,420. 18s. 11d., and
Major Andrew Coats gave £7,000.

The Reception Committee
of the
Scottish National Antarctic Expedition
requests the honour of your presence on board the Steamer
which will sail from Wemyss Bay on inst.
at o'clock, to meet and convoy the "Scotia" home
The arrangements for the day are printed on the back of
this card which will admit you and friend to the Steamer.

Offices of the Scottish Antarctic Expedition *Nicolson Street, Edinburgh.*

(Top) Original map of Laurie Island.
Note the commemoration of the *Scotia's* members and families,
and Scotland, in the naming of topographical features.

(Left) 'Abstract of Account charge and discharge'
of the Scottish National Antarctic Expedition,
from 15 January 1901 to 31 August 1905. (*SPRI*)

(Right) An invitation 'to meet and convoy
the 'Scotia' home', sent from the Scottish National Antarctic
Expedition offices, Nicolson Street, Edinburgh. (*SPRI*)

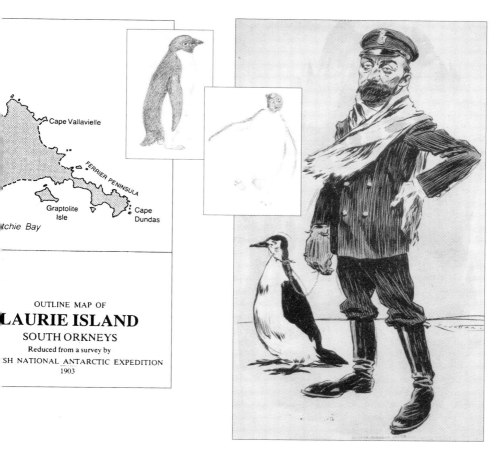

Cape Vallavielle

FERRIER PENINSULA

Graptolite
Isle

Cape
Dundas

tchie Bay

(Top, middle) Studies of Adélie penguins by William Cuthbertson (*Trustees of the National Museums of Scotland*);
(top, right) caricature of Bruce from *El Gladiator* (no. 110, January 1904) (*EUL*);
(below) quarrying fresh-water ice on Laurie Island (*Trustees of the National Museums of Scotland*)

Bruce's birthplace
at 43 Kensington Gardens Square, London.

The Bruce family house
at 18 Royal Crescent, Holland Park, London.

Bruce's house, South Morton Street (*Edinburgh University Library* [*EUL*])

open to all. Although in 1876 the leader of the Challenger Expedition, Wyville Thomson, then professor of natural history at Edinburgh University, had given a lecture comparing the characteristics of the Arctic and the Antarctic and urging a land-based expedition to Antarctica to complement *Challenger's* oceanic work, the suggestion had come to nothing. However, in 1886 the Royal Society of London recommended to the Challenger committee in Edinburgh a Joint Antarctic committee formed with interested Australian States and partly funded by the British Government in order to attract additional capital from commerce and science. (Funds were not forthcoming, although the Swedish Barons Nordenskjöld and Oscar Dickson showed interest.)

On the continent of Europe there were others who promoted scientific exploration of the high latitudes of the southern hemisphere. In 1882–83 Karl Weyprecht of the Austrian Navy initiated the first International Polar Year. Meanwhile Germany established a station on South Georgia, France built an observatory in Tierra del Fuego, and twelve countries were additionally involved on a worldwide basis with stations in both hemispheres. In 1886 the Royal Society of Edinburgh set up an Antarctic committee chaired by John Murray who had completed the Challenger reports after the death of Wyville Thomson. Murray, in an important address to the Royal Scottish Geographical Society, outlined an agenda for Antarctic exploration and, in response, the Society passed a resolution supporting, 'the careful exploration of the Antarctic Regions'.

Murray's Antarctic committee did not last long, but many of its members carried on their interests throughout the 1890s in a committee of the Royal Society of London. Important names, in addition to Murray, included Sir Erasmus Ommanney, Sir Leopold McClintock, and the president of the Royal Geographical Society, Clements Robert Markham (knighted in 1896).

Following the International Geographical Union Congress of 1891, the Royal Geographical Society and the Royal Society of London formed a joint Antarctic committee with Clements Markham as chairman. Its principal object was to promote a British Antarctic expedition (later known as the Discovery Expedition). Markham wrote subsequently of the committee: 'The worst thing I ever did was to create that Committee.'

Indeed there was to be not just one but a series of committees and joint committees established during the 1890s. A collection of Markham's letters written at this time, which candidly portrays his views of the personalities of the various committees, was edited by Clive Holland and published as *Antarctic Obsession* in 1986. It was obvious from his writing that Markham was suffering increasing frustration over the project as a whole.

In the meantime, commerce was already pointing in the direction that science was slow to follow. The 1892 Dundee Whaling Expedition, for example (see chapter 2), may have been organised primarily for commercial gain, but there was at least some attempt to carry out scientific measurements at the same time, hence the presence of Bruce and Burn Murdoch aboard *Balaena*, and Charles Donald on *Active*.

On 13 November 1893 Markham revived the subject of Antarctic exploration in his presidential address to the Royal Geographical Society:

> *The Antarctic regions, with millions of unknown square miles full of geographical work, and teeming with most interesting scientific problems, have been totally neglected by us for half a century.*

On the 27th of the same month Murray addressed the Society on 'The Renewal of Antarctic exploration', outlining in a comprehensive survey the details of scientific work to be done, both at sea and on land:

> *A dash at the South Pole is not, however what I now advocate, nor do I believe that is what British science, at the present time, desires.*

This sentiment was to lead eventually to a disagreement between Murray and Markham and to the former's later withdrawal from the project. Nonetheless in his current address Murray agreed with Markham that the Royal Navy should have charge of the polar exploration, and Dr Georg von Neumayer of the Hamburg Naval Observatory, in a written communication, stressed the need for geodetic and magnetic surveys.

At the end of the meeting the only contribution recorded from the floor came from Bruce, who rose to say:

> *I agree thoroughly ... that this expedition should be of a national character .... I am sure that there will be no difficulty in getting scientific volunteers; I for one am ready to spend a winter at one of Dr. Murray's winter stations.*

The matter of Antarctica had first been raised by Sir Erasmus Ommanney at the aforementioned Berne Conference of the International Geographical Union in 1891. Meeting every four years, the next one was scheduled to convene in London in 1895. As president of the Royal Geographical Society it fell to Markham to act as principal host and to chair the executive meetings. At its conclusion the Congress endorsed unanimously a number of resolutions, the seventh of which read:

> *That the Congress records its opinion that the exploration of the Antarctic regions is the greatest piece of geographical exploration still to be undertaken. That, in view of the additions to knowledge in almost every branch of science which would result from such a scientific exploration, the Congress recommends that the scientific societies*

throughout the world should urge in whatever way seems to them most effective, that this work should be undertaken before the close of the century.

[The resolution had been framed by the Secretary of the meeting, Dr Hugh Robert Mill.]

Although the spirit of the resolution was entirely scientific and not overtly nationalistic or commercial, the Heroic Age of Polar Exploration had effectively begun and the race for the South Pole was now underway. During this period no less than 14 national Antarctic expeditions were mounted, excluding relief expeditions and purely commercial voyages.

National Expeditions of the Heroic Age of Polar Exploration

Expedition	Ship	Leader	Date
Belgian Antarctic Expedition	*Belgica*	Adrien de Gerlache	1897-1899
British Antarctic Expedition	*Southern Cross*	Carsten Borchgrevink	1898-1900
German South Polar Expedition	*Gauss*	Erich von Drygalski	1901-1903
Swedish South Polar Expedition	*Antarctica*	Nils Otto Nordenskjöld	1901-1904
British National Antarctic Expedition	*Discovery*	Robert Falcon Scott	1901-1904
Scottish National Antarctic Expedition	*Scotia*	William Speirs Bruce	1902-1904
French Antarctic Expedition	*Francais*	Jean-Baptiste Charcot	1903-1904
British Antarctic Expedition	*Nimrod*	Ernest Henry Shackleton	1907-1909
French Antarctic Expedition	*Pourquoi-Pas*	Jean-Baptiste Charcot	1908-1910
Norwegian Antarctic Expedition	*Fram*	Roald Amundsen	1910-1912
British Antarctic Expedition	*Terra Nova*	Robert Falcon Scott	1910-1913
German South Polar Expedition	*Deutschland*	Wilhelm Filchner	1911-1912
Australian Antarctic Expedition	*Aurora*	Douglas Mawson	1911-1914
Imperial Trans-Antarctic Expedition	*Endurance*	Ernest Henry Shackleton	1914-1916

Political movements in both England and Scotland would increasingly determine that expeditions to Antarctica were predominantly patriotic and nationalist in emphasis. This was the last major part of the world still largely *terra incognita* and Britain had already made some exploratory discoveries in the area. James Clark Ross in the 1840s had demonstrated the existence of the Ross Sea and the Ross Ice Barrier and discovered the general location of the south magnetic pole. And in 1872-76 the global Challenger Expedition, although it sailed south of the Antarctic Circle for only a short period, had begun to examine the nature of the Southern Ocean, its sea floor, sea currents, and its meteorology.

The need for further scientific analyses was not in dispute, as far as Britain was concerned. However, this created underlying questions about who should fund the expeditions, who should control them, and the extent to which personnel involved should be from the nation's Navy or independent of the Admiralty or Treasury. Should scientific societies be the prime movers, or should responsibility lie with Government?

Funding was to prove a major issue. After much prevarication the Council of the Royal Geographical Society eventually decided on 12 April 1897 to send an expedition to the Antarctic and authorised Markham to raise the funds. He advised yet another joint committee:

> *It was a fatal error, but I did so under the impression that the great names of the Royal Society and the Royal Geographical Society would bring in the funds. This was a complete mistake. The coalition has been a source of worry, delays, friction and danger; and no good whatever.*

In 1898 the Royal Geographical Society offered £5000 to the scheme, Alfred Harmsworth, the newspaper proprietor, promised £5000, and by the end of the year £14,000 had been raised. It was not enough.

Then, quite unexpectedly, a fellow of the Royal Geographical Society, a wealthy London businessman called Llewellyn Longstaff, offered £25,000 towards the venture and the situation changed dramatically. On 3 July 1899 Lord Balfour indicated that HM Treasury would provide £45,000 if a similar amount could be raised privately. Markham now realised with relief that funding was virtually assured. He set about obtaining tenders for a new ship in 1899 and agreed that *Discovery* should be built in Dundee for £34,050, plus £9700 for the steam engines.

Markham then divided the Antarctic map into four quadrants and discussed them in a paper for the *Geographical Journal* (dated July 1901). He recommended that the British expedition explore the Victoria and Ross quadrants (90°E to 180°, and 180° to 90°W respectively), and the Germans the Enderby quadrant (0° to 90°E). This left the Weddell Sea quadrant (90°W to 0°) which, according to Markham, 'offers the minimum of results with the maximum of risks'.

Markham was now able to proceed with the recruitment of appropriate naval and civilian personnel for the Discovery Expedition. Robert Falcon Scott of the Royal Navy was appointed leader on 9 June 1900, and Charlie Royd his deputy on 18 June. In addition Professor J W Gregory, formerly head of the geological department at the British Museum, was recommended by the Royal Society as chief scientist in control of all civilian staff and scientific work on land. The appointment was not particularly successful, however, as Markham noted in *Antarctic Obsession*:

Clements Robert Markham (*SPRI*)

'The Expedition was exposed to the greatest danger from a determined and carefully planned intrigue for placing a geologist named Gregory in virtual command.'

The continual wrangling over who should have ultimate command – Scott or Gregory – led to many resignations from the joint committee by April 1901. Eventually Gregory himself resigned. Markham commented:

> *Gregory has cost seven hundred pounds from first to last, the result being nothing but squabbling, worry and friction. The Expedition was well rid of him, even at that price.*

Once Cyril Longhurst was made secretary to the expedition, Markham was determined to avoid any more planning by committee. But his problems were not over yet – not by a long way.

William Speirs Bruce was about to add to Markham's woes by the announcement of an independent Scottish Antarctic Expedition, bound for the unallocated Weddell Sea quadrant. It was a case of very bad timing.

Bruce had originally written to Clements Markham from Edinburgh on 15 March 1899 to offer himself as a member of the scientific staff of the Discovery Expedition:

> *Dear Sir Clements Markham*
> *I have seen announcements regarding the Antarctic Committee in 'Nature', 'Geographical Journal', and elsewhere but I am not aware that the Committee has*

yet asked candidates to apply for the leadership or other scientific posts. I wish to let you know that I am at any time prepared to accompany the British National Antarctic Expedition should the Committee of the Royal Society and Royal Geographical Society consider me worthy. I shall be very glad to send in a formal application accompanied by testimonials.

For the past seven years I have been training myself with a view of making myself more efficient for Polar Service. I have spent one summer in the Antarctic Regions, three summers and one winter in the Arctic Regions, and more than a year on the summit of Ben Nevis in charge of the Observatory. I am a ski-runner and have taken part in sledging expeditions.

In addition to my ordinary University training in Mathematics, Physics, Chemistry, Botany, Zoology, Human Anatomy, Physiology, and Embryology, I have served in the Challenger Office under Dr. (now Sir) John Murray; as Demonstrator in Botany in the University of Edinburgh; and as Demonstrator and afterwards Assistant in Zoology in the School of Medicine of the Royal Colleges of Surgeons and Physicians.

I have contributed papers to various scientific societies including the Royal Geographical Society, Royal Scottish Geographical Society, (of which I am a Fellow), British Association, Royal Physical Society, Edinburgh (of which I am Honorary Assistant Secretary, Dr. Ramsay Traquair being Secretary) and others; also to the 'Ibis', 'Nature', and other scientific periodicals.

As naturalist to the Jackson-Harmsworth Polar Expedition I brought back collections four or five times as great as any previous expedition. During the past two winters I have been working at these in conjunction with specialists at home and abroad. In addition I have been working in a similar manner on almost equally large collections obtained by me on Mr. Andrew Coats' Yacht Blencathra in the Barentz Sea. His Serene Highness the Prince of Monaco also entrusted me with conducting the Hensen Quantitative Plankton work and Salinity Observations in his yacht Princesse Alice during his voyage last year to the Barentz and Greenland Seas. On the same occasion I took part in trawling and sounding operations in depths of nearly 2000 fathoms.

I shall be in London at the end of next week till about the 25th or 26th inst., in connection with the Zoological and Geological work of the Jackson-Harmsworth and the Andrew Coats' Arctic expeditions and should like to call on you regarding future Antarctic work at any time or place most convenient to you.

I remain,
Yours faithfully
Wm. S. Bruce

Bruce had made out a good case for serious consideration by Markham, and indeed it is unlikely that there was any other person in the British Isles at that time better qualified to be offered a place on the Discovery Expedition.

On 17 April Markham sent the following reply to Bruce:

21 Eccleston Square S.W.

Dear Mr. Bruce
I shall be glad to see you when you come to London. We have not yet taken any steps about the personnel of the Expedition.
Ever
Yours very truly,
Clements R. Markham

Bruce failed to see Markham in London, but a message was sent to him via Dr Koettlitz, who had worked with Bruce on the Jackson–Harmsworth Expedition, asking Bruce to apply for an assistant's place on the expedition. Bruce accordingly sent the following on 21 March 1900, almost a year after his original note of interest:

Dear Sir Clements Markham
I have to thank you for the message you have conveyed me through Dr. Koettlitz. I have already lodged my application to become a member of the British Antarctic Expedition, which you were good enough to acknowledge on the 17th April last year. I forget if I gave any names as references so I now mention seven gentlemen who know me and whom I am asking to act as references, viz:
*   H.S.H. The Prince of Monaco*
*   Sir John Murray, K.C.B., F.R.S.*
*   Dr. Alexander Buchan, F.R.S.*
*   Dr. Fridtjof Nansen*
*   Mr. Andrew Coats*
*   Mr. Alfred Harmsworth*

And then the bombshell …

I may say I am not without hopes of being able to raise sufficient capital whereby I could take out a second British ship to explore in the Antarctic Regions.
*   I remain,*
*   Yours very truly*
*   Wm. S. Bruce*

Three days later, Bruce wrote again to Markham to tell him about money that he had been promised by supporters of the Scottish expedition:

… In my letter of the 21st. inst. I stated that I had expectations of being able to raise sufficient capital for a second British ship. I now send you yesterday's 'Scotsman'

and 'Evening Dispatch' in which there are reports and reviews of my plans. I am glad to say that I have already met with very considerable success, and believe the sending of a second ship is now assured. I consider it important that the work of the Scottish Expedition should be complementary to and co-operative with that of the German and British Expeditions.

I remain,
Yours very truly
Wm. S. Bruce

However, the prospect of another expedition had angered Markham. The Royal Geographical Society was still finalising the funding for the British Antarctic Expedition and Markham was worried that the Scottish venture might gain media exposure at the expense of the British one. Even though Bruce had stressed that he saw the Scottish expedition as complementary to *Discovery* ('a second British ship,' as Bruce called it) and entirely within the spirit of the International Geographical Union resolution, Markham felt compelled to write a letter to Bruce in a tone of petulance that served only to encourage him and the other promoters of the Scottish expedition to consolidate their plans. Markham's letter was dated 23 March, the day before Bruce's confirmation of the initiation of a Scottish expedition, but it had been delayed by a wrong address and was not received by Bruce until 26 March.

Dear Mr. Bruce

I am very sorry to hear that an attempt is to be made in Edinburgh to divert funds from the Antarctic Expedition in order to get up a rival enterprise. Such a course will be most prejudicial to the Expedition which is much in need of more funds. A second ship is not in the least required. It is not true that the whole area is not provided for. If the Germans do not undertake the Weddell Quadrant, it will be undertaken by our Expedition as a first object. I do not understand why this mischievous rivalry should have been started, but I trust that you will not connect yourself with it.

Markham's views served to alienate many members of the joint committee of the Royal Geographical Society and the Royal Society that had been formed to promote the British Antarctic Expedition. The Scottish members, in particular John Young Buchanan, were already becoming irritated that Markham, rather than the committee, was making all the important decisions. The Scottish scientific establishment, therefore, began to look favourably upon the prospect of a Scottish expedition, particularly as they had in Bruce the most experienced polar researcher in Britain to act as its leader. Murray, at that time president of the Royal Scottish Geographical Society, gave the first intimation to the council that money might be forthcoming for a Scottish expedition at its meeting held on 22 March 1900 after Bruce had told him that he believed he could raise between £35,000 and £40,000. The council of the Society gave its blessing to the enterprise.

In the June 1900 issue of the *Scottish Geographical Magazine*, Bruce outlined his plans in detail, indicating that he had support from Murray and the leader of the German (Gauss) Expedition, Professor Erich von Drygalski. The Scottish expedition would complement the others and sail via Port Stanley for the Weddell Sea, leaving on 1 August 1901. It would endeavour to establish a wintering station as far south as possible, even to 80°S. He added, 'no unnecessary sacrifice of the ship, or of scientific work and records [would] be made, however, in attempting to reach the South Pole, but failing to find land south, a course will be steered eastwards to strike the southern continuation of Graham's Land, where the station will be set up'.

Bruce meanwhile, at a loss to explain Markham's outburst, wrote back by return:

> ... *I do not understand why you should look upon my Expedition to the Weddell Sea as a rival to the British Antarctic Expedition. If my friends are prepared to give me money to carry out my plans, I do not see why I should not accept it, neither do I see why I should not accept the patronage and advice of any of the scientific societies, in the event of my departure.*
>
> *There are at present no less than five Scientific expeditions wintering in the very much explored Arctic Regions, working in friendly co-operation. I do not see how there cannot be room for my small expedition in addition to the German and British Expeditions, in the very much unexplored Antarctic regions. With regard to a second ship not being in the least required, this is a point upon which authorities differ, there are several who maintain that a second ship is highly desirable.*
>
> *I am very sorry that you should look upon my efforts as mischievous rivalry. Perhaps my letter of the 24th inst, which has crossed yours will show that I am not working as a rival.*
>
> *Ever, Yours very truly*
> *Wm. S. Bruce*

Markham replied, also by return, in no way conciliatory and certainly not accepting Bruce's explanation. His letter, dated 27 March, points out:

> ... *as you are a volunteer for the Antarctic Expedition, and as you know I was doing my best to get you appointed, I certainly had a right to think that you would not take such a step as you have done, without at least consulting me ....*

[Bruce subsequently wrote across the letter, 'I wasted over a year with no remit'.]

Markham continued:

> *The Weddell Quadrant has been fully provided for. If the Germans do not undertake it, as I understand from Drygalski, certainly the British Expedition will.*

In fact the instructions given to Scott had no provision for examining the Weddell quadrant. Nor was this attempted:

> *Of course a whaler, fitted out for scientific work, may be useful; but it would be far better to have one expedition well supplied with funds, than two insufficiently supplied and I regret your action – suddenly sprung upon me without a word of consultation.*

On 16 May 1900 Markham returned to his correspondence with Bruce, indicating that he had received a letter from von Drygalski who asserted that the Weddell quadrant had been agreed with Markham in Berlin as part of the German sphere of action. Bruce pencilled a note: 'This is contrary to my communication with Drygalski.' Markham added:

> *When I said a second ship was not wanted, I intended to refer to an independent ship. Of course a second ship for the expedition would be, in the opinion of many people a great advantage; but I am afraid that is not what you intend. You will cripple the National Expedition which is actually on foot, in order to get up a scheme for yourself.*

Bruce replied, saying that the Scottish expedition would aid and add to the value of the British National Expedition, and in an addendum only for his close associates, he scribbled:

> *The Coats family who gave me over £30,000 would not have subscribed this to the other project. It was therefore all additional money for Antarctic Research.*

Although Bruce was later offered a place on the Discovery Expedition by Markham, the Scottish venture was by now too far advanced for Bruce to consider it. He was already recruiting for his own expedition. In a letter of 14 February 1901, Markham finally adopted a conciliatory tone:

> *Dear Mr. Bruce*
> *I am afraid I replied rather angrily when you announced your expedition to me: for I feared that your proceedings would divert funds from the national expedition*

which was and is much in need. But I can now see things from your point of view; and wish you success. Mr. Armitage tells me that you have been married, and I send my congratulations on the happy event.

I shall be at Dundee in March for the launching of the Discovery; *and I hope I shall see you then ....*

Bruce had already begun to prepare for his expedition and set his sights on a ship. He looked first of all at the *Balaena* in Dundee, but it was too expensive, so he sought the advice of Colin Archer in Norway who had built Fridtjof Nansen's famous *Fram*. Bruce and Archer selected a Norwegian whaler, *Hekla*, which Bruce purchased for £2620. Formerly it had been managed by the Norwegian Antarctic explorer, Henryk Johan Bull.

Superficially the ship appeared to be in good condition. It was sailed to Scotland and navigated through the Caledonian Canal, with only one foot to spare on each side in the loch gates, to the yards of the Ailsa Shipbuilding Company at Troon, Ayrshire. On detailed examination, however, it became evident that *Hekla* required a complete overhaul.

Although the re-fit substantially increased costs to £16,730.12s.10d., it allowed the naval architect, G L Watson, who provided his services entirely free, to incorporate all the improvements Bruce required for an oceanographic voyage to the Antarctic. Bruce used his experiences aboard *Princesse Alice* and from his work with the Challenger collections to design the best possible research ship within his budget. The *Hekla*, renamed appropriately *Scotia,* was turned into a fine vessel, with excellent individual rooms for the captain and scientific staff, good crew quarters, and purpose-built laboratories.

The re-fit costs meant that more fundraising was required and this delayed the expedition's departure from the original plan of 1 August, designed to make the most of the Antarctic summer. By August, however, the ship was only ready for trials. Encouragingly it achieved a speed of over eight knots on a measured mile and, according to Mill, it was 'the most graceful of all the exploring ships'.

Bruce was anxious to maximise the use of the ship in open sea and not to allow it to become frozen in the ice during the southern winter. He was also hoping the scientists would have provisions for three winters in a shore-based hut. In the November 1901 *Scottish Geographical Magazine*, Bruce reported that he had enough money for one ship and 30 men, of whom eight would be scientific staff. He repeated that the work would be primarily oceanographic, geological and meteorological and submitted written comments from the eminent German scientists Professor von Richtofen, Professor Erich von Drygalski, Carl Chung, A Sprung and Karl Brandt. Even Nansen added an appeal to Scotsmen to 'enable the equipment and scale of the Expedition to be a credit to Scotland and an ornament to Science'.

Re-fitting *Hekla* to become *Scotia* in dry dock at Ailsa Shipbuilding Company yards, Troon. (*RSGS*)

The money for the expedition came principally from the Coats family of Paisley. In 1900 James Coats Junior contributed £14,000 initially, and his brother Major Andrew Coats, with whom Bruce had sailed in *Blencathra*, added £7000. In 1901 James donated a further sum – just over £9000 – in order that *Scotia* should spend a second winter in Antarctica. Including additional provisions supplied by James Coats, such as Fair Isle sweaters, the extent of the family's contribution was £30,000 out of a total cost of £36,405. Sums of money and gifts in kind from smaller donors were also received and acknowledgement of 170 firms and individuals was given in the *Scottish Geographical Magazine* for November 1903, the majority of the sponsors coming from within Scotland.

Specialised equipment came from other scientists: the Prince of Monaco provided deep-sea appliances; John Young Buchanan supplied a thermometer and hydrometers; the Astronomer Royal of Scotland provided a theodolite and ship's telescope 'of very fine quality'; Alfred Harmsworth donated a chronometer, aneroid barometer and sledges; the British Admiralty provided hydrographic instruments and charts; the Treasury supplied the voluminous

Challenger reports; the German Government similarly provided the Valdivia reports of 1898-99; and the Belgian Government sent the Belgica reports of 1897-99. Altogether it was an auspicious start.

In the Ship's Agreement (Ref: Public Record Office – BT 100/292A 8127), the Managing Owner is described as James Coats of Ferguslie House, Paisley, and the number of seamen as 35 (*ie* the maximum number of seamen for whom accommodation is certified). SY *Scotia* was described as '… on a voyage from Troon to the South Polar Regions calling at any ports or places required on a voyage of discovery and scientific research, the voyage not to exceed three years. The service of crew to terminate in the United Kingdom within the period stated.'

At the annual meeting of the British Association held in Belfast in September 1901, Bruce outlined his plans. The expedition was now to be called the Scottish National Antarctic Expedition, and a ship, *Scotia*, was currently being rebuilt for the purpose. It was a barque-rigged auxiliary screw steamer about 400 tons, length 140 feet (42.7m), breadth 29 feet (8.8m), drawing 15 feet (4.6m) of water. Amidships the planking was 25 inches (64cm) and there would be two well-equipped laboratories, a dark room, and a Lucas sounding machine with two drums of 6000 cable each. Bruce had profited well from his experiences aboard *Princesse Alice*.

The ship's officers and crew were appointed, as set out below. As mentioned previously, Captain Thomas Robertson was taken on as master of *Scotia*:

The Officers

Name	Age	Address	Position
Thomas Robertson	48	Prosen Cottage, Newport, Fifeshire	Captain
Robert Davidson	40	8 Graham Place, Dundee	Second mate; icemaster
James McDougall	37	145 Princess Street, Dundee	Third mate and bo'sun
John Fitchie	53	237 Blackness Road, Dundee	Promoted from third to first mate in Stanley
Bryce Allan Thomson	28	Alva Villa, Tobermory	First mate; left ship in Stanley, Jan 1903
Henry Anderson	26	4 Parker's Court, Dundee	Able seaman
Alexander Duncan	29	1 Constitution Street, Peterhead	Fireman
Edwin Florence	28	22 Queen Street, Peterhead	Chief cook; promoted to first steward, Buenos Aires, Jan 1904
Henry Gravill	28	93 Arbroath Road, Dundee	Second Engineer; promoted to Chief engineer after death of Allan Ramsay

The Company

Name	Age	Address	Position
Andrew Greig	22	Dagleish Street, Tayport, Fife	AB; left ship in Buenos Aires, Jan 1904
Gilbert Kerr	32	241 Causewayside, Edinburgh	Ordinary seaman, Laboratory assistant, piper
David Low	42	40 Lilybank Road, Dundee	Fireman
John Macmurchie	28	17 Laurimer Street, Dundee	AB; left ship in Buenos Aires, Jan 1904
Thomas Mackenzie	38	20 West Princess Street, Rothesay	Chief steward; discharged due to sickness, Buenos Aires, Jan 1904
James McKenzie	24	59 Wellgate, Dundee	AB; left ship in Buenos Aires, Jan 1903
Robert McKenzie	23	29 Wellgate, Dundee	AB; discharged for misconduct, Buenos Aires, Jan 1904
William Martin	26	42 Step Road, Dundee	AB; signed over to scientific staff, Omond House, Oct 1903 to Feb 1904
William Murray	30	Stirling Village, Boddam, Aberdeenshire	Promoted to chief cook from 2nd cook, Buenos Aires, Jan 1904
David Patrick	38	10 Church Street, Dundee	Bo'sun and quarryman; shipped in Buenos Aires, Jan 1903
Allan Ramsay	25	6 Wellington Street, Dundee	First engineer; died on board 6 August 1903
James Rice	42	East Union Street, Troon	Carpenter; left ship in Buenos Aires, Jan 1904
Alexander Robertson	46	1 Caith Street, Peterhead	AB; left ship in Buenos Aires, January 1904
James Smith	21	1 Middle Street, Dundee	AB; carpenter's mate; left ship in Buenos Aires, 1904
John Smith ('Shetland Johnnie')	21	East Wharf, Shetland,	Ordinary seaman
William Smith	42	2 St Matthew Street	Second steward; remained as cook at Omond House, 27 Nov 1903 to 1 Jan 1905
A J Walker	28	13 Sea Gate, Peterhead	AB; skinman and lampman
Robert Wilson	22	11 Armour Street, Kilmarnock	Fireman and blacksmith

It is evident from the crew list that Bruce had concentrated on recruitment in Scotland. On the whole his men were used to sailing around the world from Scottish ports and some had considerable experience of icy waters and whaling voyages. However *Scotia* did recruit during the voyage: in Buenos Aires a Uruguayan, Carlos Haymes, was enlisted to replace Allan Ramsay as chief engineer; and Thomas Fraser joined the ship as carpenter in Cape Town on the homeward-bound leg of the journey.

Bruce appointed the scientific staff himself: they were already his friends or had worked with him in the field. They comprised Rudmose Brown, recently graduated from the University of Aberdeen, as botanist; Robert Cockburn Mossman of Edinburgh as meteorologist; James H Harvey Pirie as medical doctor and geologist; David W Wilton, a fellow participant in the Jackson–Harmsworth Expedition; with two untrained assistants, Alastair Ross as taxidermist, and William Cuthbertson as artist.

Finally, in addition to the men, Bruce brought along a Samoyed dog called 'Russ', or 'Sir John' after Sir John Murray, and he bought eleven collie dogs in the Falkland Islands.

All the expedition members had to sign a legal document with Bruce, setting out the terms of their contract in which he claimed the rights 'to publish and hold copyright of all observations, memoranda, plans, sketches and positive photographs for a period of one year from the date of the return to Great Britain of the said expedition'.

The organisation of the Scottish National Antarctic Expedition was now complete. The expedition's offices were at 21 Hill Place, Edinburgh, with James Ferrier a most efficient secretary, and Thomas B Whitson, accountant, as treasurer.

The objects of the expedition and the qualifications of the scientific staff were published in the *Scottish Geographical Magazine* and the same information published in London in the *Geographical Journal* for October 1902:

> *To set up a wintering station for three years as near to the South Pole as is practicable.*
>
> *To fit out a ship, to land the wintering party, and to carry on deep sea and other research in the Antarctic Ocean to the south of South America.*
>
> *To carry on systematic observations and researches in Meteorology, Geology, Biology, Topography, and Terrestrial Physics.*

The expedition members were given a splendid farewell dinner by Sir John Murray on behalf of the Royal Scottish Geographical Society on Thursday 23 October 1902 at the North British Station Hotel, Edinburgh. It was a dinner in the grand Edwardian style, starting with a dish of oysters, followed by consommé or creamed soup, supreme of sole or whiting, a

Members of the Scotia Expedition (from left to right):
standing — Ferrier (secretary), Rudmose Brown, Harvey Pirie, Ross, Cuthbertson, Whitson (treasurer);
sitting — Mossman, Bruce, Robertson, Wilton (and Russ — Sir John, the dog). (*SPRI*)

sorbet, saddle of salted beef, partridge with salad, a soufflé and ice creams, savouries and coffee.

Murray spoke highly of Bruce, touching on the dissension in the London committee: 'Scotland was to have an expedition of her own, because they had still a Bruce in Scotland.' He continued:

> *I should like to emphasise the fact that all those who had been shipmates with Mr. Bruce, and those who had worked with him on the top of Ben Nevis, had formed a very high opinion of his abilities and capabilities.*

On the eve of departure *The Scotsman* newspaper featured an article about the expedition expressing with pride its national character:

> *The enterprise may be described as a national one: the leader and all the scientific and nautical members of the expedition are Scots; the funds have been collected for the most part on this side of the Border; it is the product of voluntary effort, and unlike the expedition which will be simultaneously employed in the exploration of the Antarctic, it owes nothing to Government help.*

Members of the *Scotia* Expedition aboard ship. *(Peter Wordie)*

The writer continued in the same vein:

> *The Antarctic may seem to narrow-souled and unimaginative people a barren field in which to squander effort and money. To wider and more generous apprehension the £25000 or £30000 expended on the Scotia Expedition will seem a good national investment, even should only a part of the programme of the voyage be fulfilled. To the members of the little party who set out so courageously to grapple with the great and unknown faces of the Southern Ocean and the southern cold, Scotland and Science bid a hearty 'God-speed'.*

References

Baughman, T H: *Before the Heroes Came* (Lincoln, Nebraska and London, 1994).

Markham, Clements Robert: *Antarctic Obsession* (editor Clive Holland) (Alburgh, 1986).

Mill, Hugh Robert: *Siege of the South Pole* (London, 1905).

Yelverton, David E: *Antarctica Unveiled: Scott's First Expedition and the Quest for the Unknown Continent* (Boulder: University Press of Colorado, 2000).

CHAPTER 7

THE SCOTIA EXPEDITION

The Scotia, *of the Scottish National Antarctic Expedition, sailed yesterday from Troon .... By the courtesy of the Glasgow and South-Western Railway Company, the tug* Titchfield, *carrying a large party of interested spectators, accompanied the* Scotia, *which steamed rapidly towards her escort the* Gleniffer *(on which was the owner Mr Coats, Mr G. L. Watson, the designer of* Scotia; *and Messrs Ferrier and Whitson) and* Triton .... *The* Scotia, *amid the waving of hankerchiefs and the strains of the pipes, steamed off on her long voyage.*

SO recorded the local press about *Scotia's* departure from Troon for the Weddell Sea and Antarctica on the morning of 2 November 1902. *Gleniffer* and *Triton* accompanied the ship as far as Kingstown (Dun Laoghaire), the outport for Dublin. At Kingstown Bruce was presented with two barrels of porter by the Irish brewing company Messrs Guinness, a keen supporter of the expedition. With only a modest budget Bruce had given priority to the purchase of food, chemicals and scientific equipment, so Coats generously supplied the ship from his own stocks of tobacco and spirits.

Scotia journeyed south, calling at Funchal, the port for Madeira, to take on water and a gift of coal from the Union Castle Line; thence to Cape Verde Isles, before making an abortive attempt to land members of the expedition on the dangerous St Paul's Rocks. They reached Port Stanley in the Falkland Islands on 6 January 1903. After three weeks of further provisioning, the ship set sail for Antarctica on 26 January, and by 3 February the South Orkney Islands were sighted. The vessel began to encounter the first flurries of snow and pack ice.

Bruce and some of the other scientists made a brief landing on Saddle Island to collect specimens of penguins, sheath bills, skuas, giant petrels, rocks and eggs, before Captain Robertson steered the ship back into open water until 70°S was reached on 23 February. Dredging was now begun, as well as sounding the ocean depths (one depth reading of 2543 fathoms was secured), taking hourly meteorological readings and, as conditions allowed, boarding icebergs to replenish the water tanks.

But the summer season was nearing its end. To be trapped and crushed

Scotia frozen in the ice, Scotia Bay, Laurie Island. *(SPRI)*

in the ice in the Weddell Sea was a real danger – a fate that later befell Shackleton's ship *Endurance* – so a sheltered place to overwinter was sought.

Bruce had to abandon all hope of getting further south. Instead it was decided to find a sheltered bay and to allow *Scotia* to become ice-bound over winter. Captain Robertson negotiated the ship along the edge of the ice back to the South Orkney Islands and by 21 March they found a suitable harbour on the south side of Laurie Island where the ship was allowed to become frozen into the ice at the place they called Scotia Bay. The Bay was partially sheltered from storms coming from the west and *Scotia* was positioned only 500 yards (457m) from a good landing on The Beach. She was destined to remain here until released by the spring thawing of the sea ice on 27 November 1903.

Throughout this period Bruce pursued a disciplined programme of scientific work. In addition to meteorological readings there were regular trawls and dredges made through holes cut in the ice, and occasional collection of eggs and rock samples. A fire hole, a necessary precaution, was situated near the bow of the ship and kept clear of ice for access to water in an emergency. A cable was laid between the fire hole and another hole set

Laurie Island Meteorological Station – Omond House. (*SPRI*)

some distance away, and this was used to operate the dredge throughout the winter.

On The Beach a start was made in the construction of a scientific station they named Omond House after Robert Traill Omond, director of the Edinburgh Observatory, a major supporter of the expedition who had supplied simple plans for its construction. Omond House was built as a residence for the party that would be left on Laurie Island the following summer when *Scotia* went for a re-fit. The scientific instruments were on arrays close by.

Unlike some other polar expeditions, Bruce had insufficient funds to take with him a prefabricated structure to erect on the land. Instead the carpenter provided main beams from the ship's timber supplies and the crew were set to quarry from the frozen ground a sufficient supply of rocks to build the walls in the manner of a Scottish bothy. The dry-stone construction was then packed with pebbles and snow which froze in the low temperatures to improve the insulation and stability of the house. The interior of the walls and door were lined with canvas, with hammocks slung inside and two beds.

Rudmose Brown, in letters home to his parents, described the building of the house in some detail:

> *The biggest job of all was building a house for the summer party of six people to live in for two or three months. It is 20 feet square, built of rough stones, fitted together*

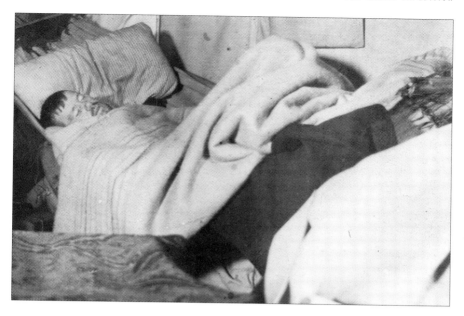

Sleeping quarters inside Omond House. (RSGS)

into walls two to four feet thick and roofed with wood and an old sail; with two windows and a door and an outside porch. The floor is covered with thick planks, ripped out of the lower deck and the main hold and finished off with bits of boxes. The inside is lined throughout with new canvas and the galley stove is to be left in place of a temporary one we have rigged up at present. Outside is a shed of biscuit boxes [ship's biscuits were packed in tins, covered in wood] *and roofed with a sail. This is for provisions and coals. Food and coals for 12 months or more is being left in case of any delay in our return to pick up the party left here. All of us helped to build: either digging the foundations, fetching stones or fitting them together. And considering that we had no mortar and no masons' tools it is a wonderfully fine house and very lasting. I should think it will be standing a century hence as a record of our hard winter's work.*

We have already done biological work also. Every day we dredge over a hundred yards of ground by means of holes kept open for the purpose. That is always done the first thing after breakfast. Then we have made holes in the ice in various places and let down traps. These are visited every other day. It often falls to my lot to super-intend the lifting of them.

Omond House, the principal building, although now a ruin, survives as the oldest of the historic huts of the Heroic Age, together with others that are better known, such as Captain Scott's hut on Ross Island. The general site of Omond House, however, is still in continuous use. After the Scottish

Living quarters in Omond House, with Bill Smith the cook. (RSGS)

expedition returned home, a joint Scottish–Argentinian party continued the readings on behalf of the Argentinian Meteorological Service, and Argentina has now replaced it with its own modern station, Orcadas.

The South Orkney Islands were probably first discovered by the sealer, George Powell of London in 1821, sailing in *Dove*, and shortly afterwards by the American, N B Palmer, in *James Munroe*. In the same year the Scottish whaler James Weddell rediscovered them and charted the island group in 1823, landing on both Saddle and Coronation Islands and naming them after the Orkney Islands in Scotland. Ostensibly they remained *terra nullius,* or 'no-man's land', until formally annexed in 1908 by the British Government as a Dependency of the Falkland Islands. The South Orkney Islands are a mountainous group of islands, 85 per cent covered by glaciers and uninhabited these days except for the Orcadas station and a summer scientific station operated by the British Antarctic Survey on Signy Island.

The *Scotia*'s company soon developed a daily routine of scientific work, replenishing the water supply from fresh snow and land ice, building Omond House and, for recreation, ski-running across the pack ice and down nearby glaciers. Traps were set that yielded up to 60 fish a day, mostly served at breakfast, and penguins were captured for fresh meat. A store of frozen penguin was laid down in the autumn. Occasionally a seal was killed to vary the diet, but it was never appreciated as much as penguin meat. The crew of *Scotia* remained well fed and very healthy throughout the expedition.

Frozen Guinness. (*Glasgow University Archive*)

In the winter, daylight faded around 3.00pm and all activities were confined to the ship: they played games, read from the library of general literature, and occasionally entertained each other with amateur theatricals. The piper, Gilbert Kerr, played traditional Scottish airs around the deck each evening. On special occasions, such as birthdays and other memorable dates, the Captain would order spirits for celebratory drinks.

On Midwinter Day (24 June 1903), the shortest day of the year, the crew's morale, like the mercury in the thermometers, had fallen to a low level. The contribution from Messrs Guinness that day was much appreciated, as Bruce recorded in the ship's Log:

> *We opened a barrel of porter, one of two that Messrs Guinness presented to the ship at Dublin. After we had run off a certain amount it stopped running and on opening the head of the cask we found that the rest had frozen solidly. The part we drew off was excessively strong, the watery part having frozen and left the alcohol. We did not discover this until a number of the crew had been served with it, and several of them were quite drunk. The unwonted hilarity this occasioned caused this day to be long remembered, and was named by the crew 'the night of the porter supper'.*

Throughout the expedition Bruce took the early morning watch, 4.00am to 8.00am, read the scientific instruments, and wrote the Log (which remained unpublished until 1992). He took great interest in the welfare of his men, especially the youngest crew member, 'Shetland Johnnie', just 21 years of age. In the evenings Bruce would give him lessons in arithmetic and reading. Bruce records in the Log for 20 July 1903:

There have been tiffs between different members of the expedition, and between myself and certain members. But, I think, as Mossman does, that we have been singularly free from such incidents. Everybody has tried to forget and forgive, to give and take, and to acknowledge by his actions that perhaps he has been as liable to error as his temporary opponent. By their very perseverance to do more work than any other expedition in the field, all show that the welfare of the expedition is really first in their thoughts. Besides a good record of solid work in whatever capacity we may act, it is my wish that each one should be able to feel in after life that not only did he person-ally help the work of the expedition, but that that work helped and educated him. I would like them to regard the ship as their university, as their alma mater *in the highest possible sense. Not an institution given up in any way to getting through examinations, but one in which they will be able to study the various phenomena of Nature, without bias, from Nature itself: and learn that they, as well as their fellows, have many shortcomings which each should seek to overcome. I am here as leader rather than commander, in order to guide and correct the work of the various individuals, so that its aggregate may be of the greatest possible value to science and the world.*

The ship was kept warm by the stove and was well insulated by banks of snow piled up around the hull. In the sub-zero temperatures outside there was little chance of bacteria incubating and this, along with the diet of fresh fish and penguin meat, contributed to the excellent health of the party through-out the entire expedition. Allan Ramsay, the chief engineer, was the tragic exception. Suffering from a heart complaint that remained undiagnosed before he left Scotland, Ramsay had only shown signs of being unwell by the time they reached the Falklands, but considered it his duty to stay with the expedition rather than return home. But as winter progressed he grew weaker and gave great anxiety to Bruce and the doctor, Harvey Pirie. On 6 August 1903 it was clear that Ramsay was dying, and Bruce described the sad event in his Log thus:

Ramsay had a very bad night. At 6.30 a.m. I woke Ross and Willie, who had some breakfast, and left the ship at daylight, about 7 a.m., to tell Pirie to return at once, and to help Brown and Martin to pack up and follow. MacMurchie followed with the dogs. Pirie arrived very quickly, being on board about 9.50 a.m. Ramsay was very far gone by then, and had bid good-bye to all. He thanked me for my kindness to him, and asked me to stay with him to the last. Pirie administered sulphonal and morphine, as well as strychnine, after which he slept for five hours, his breathing and heart improving all the time. At five or ten minutes past three he woke again. I saw a change. Pirie had not returned. I stepped out of my berth for a second and quickly told Willie to find Pirie. Pirie was at the gangway, and was present in a minute. A further injection of strychnine was of no avail. Ramsay held out his hand feebly, and said, 'Goodbye, I'm dying,' and in another two minutes or less all was over. Pirie had his hand on his heart, and 'Hands off' were the last words he said. It was 3.14 p.m. when I looked at my watch just after he died. Pirie, the captain and I carried his body to his own berth, and the Scottish Standard half-mast high announced the sad news to all.

Ramsay was buried on the North Beach with all crew present. The piper played the 'The Flowers o' the Forest' lament and 'The Old Hundredth'. He was laid to rest with his face 'looking to the sun, northward and homeward'.

Along The Beach two other structures were erected. The first, Copeland House, was a seven and a half foot square of space for Mossman to carry out his magnetic observations. It was named after Professor Ralph Copeland of Edinburgh, the Astronomer Royal, and constructed entirely of wood. The other structure, The Cairn, was nine feet high by eight feet across (2.7m x 2.4m) and acted as a flagstaff displaying the Union Jack and the Saltire. Its main function, however, was as a fixed point from which to take survey readings.

As spring approached it was possible to explore further afield. The dogs pulled sledging parties to complete a trigonometrical survey of Laurie Island, the work being done mainly by Bruce, Rudmose Brown, Wilton and Harvey Pirie. Bruce added topographical names to the map commemorating family, friends and supporters back home, but he never added his own. At the same time he was building a photographic record with his verascope (for taking stereoscopic images), conventional cameras, and experimenting with a cine-camera, one of the earliest to be used in the Antarctic. Although some cine-film has survived, Bruce had a great deal of trouble with the camera, and also with making sound recordings of the wildlife. Not one of the recordings has been traced.

As daylengths increased, birds returned to the island in profusion; some five million penguins, mainly adelies and gentoos, and flocks of skuas, petrels, sheathbills, cormorants and Cape pigeons. Rudmose Brown wrote of Laurie Island: 'Of course there are prettier places and more sympathetic places, but I doubt if any more absolutely beautiful.'

On 23 November the wind blew from the east, breaking the pack and freeing *Scotia* from her long winter berth. Captain Robertson headed for open water and made a course for the Falklands. Left behind at Omond House were Mossman, in charge of the scientific station, together with Harvey Pirie, Cuthbertson, Ross, Martin and William Smith as cook.

Port Stanley was reached on 2 December and on 8 December *Scotia* sailed for Buenos Aires. (Bruce himself went ahead of *Scotia* aboard a faster mail steamer to make arrangements for *Scotia*'s arrival.) In the capital they were given a warm welcome by the Argentine and the British communities. The Argentine Navy granted free dry docking for the ship and well-wishers provided food and clothing, even wine and flowers.

Members of *Scotia* had already enjoyed news from home when they stopped at the Falklands: they heard how *Discovery* was held fast in the ice of McMurdo Sound; about the disappearance of the Swedish *Antarctic* and the subsequent rescue by the Argentine vessel, *Uruguay*; and about the return home of von Drygalski's *Gauss*. Bruce in return was now able to report a highly-successful oceanographical voyage of 4000 miles (6437km) of hitherto unexplored ocean, trawling to depths of 2700 fathoms at 70°S, 17°W, the erection of a scientific station, Omond House, and a survey of Laurie Island.

In Buenos Aires, Bruce sought out the British minister, W H D Haggard, the British Consul, Carnegie Ross, the director of the Argentine Meteorological Office, Dr Walter G Davis, and Dr Francisco Moreno, director of La Plata Museum. He was received by the vice president of the country, Señor Escalente, and the president himself, Dr Julio Roca. Bruce was anxious that the work at Omond House should continue after the expedition had returned to Scotland. In a spate of correspondence it became clear that neither the Foreign Office nor the Admiralty in London had any interest in the South Orkney Islands, and had no objection to Bruce handing over the station to Argentina. Evan MacGregor, the under secretary of state of the Foreign Office, wrote to Bruce on 26 March 1904:

> *I am commanded by my Lords Commissioners of the Admiralty to acknowledge the receipt of your letter of the 5th instant relative to the suggestion made by the Argentine Press that the Argentine Government should take possession of the South Orkneys, and enquiring if their Lordships are disposed to offer any remarks as to their value to this country.*
>
> *In reply I am to request that you will inform the Marquess of Lansdowne that they do not attach any importance to the possession of these islands from a naval point of view. The South Orkneys are a desolate group of rocky islands lying about 600 miles South East of the Falkland Islands and are ice-bound for the greater part of the year. Though they were discovered in 1821 by a British sealer, their Lordships are not aware that His Majesty's Government has ever laid claim to them, nor does it appear that they would ever be of any value, unless gold or other valuable minerals were discovered there or the fur seals were again to become abundant.*

At no time did Bruce contemplate recommending a wholesale transfer of the island archipelago to Argentina; he was concerned solely with the continuation of the meteorological, magnetic, and biological work on Laurie Island, as this letter of 19 January 1904 from Walter Davis shows:

> *In confirmation of our verbal arrangements for the continuance of the magnetic and meteorological observations at Scotia Bay in the South Orkney Islands by the Argentine Government, in accordance with the ministerial decree accepting your proposal to convey the observers designated for this work to Scotia Bay, I have the honour to submit to you the following:–*
>
> *It is to be hoped that Mr. Robert C. Mossman will remain in charge of the station at Scotia Bay but in the employ of the Argentine Government.*
>
> *… The men selected as assistant observers for the Scotia Bay Station are,*
> > *Edgar C. Szmula*
> > *Luciano H. Valette*
> > *Hugo Acuna*
>
> *… I take this opportunity of expressing my sincere acknowledgement of your kindness and generosity in placing at the disposal of this department the buildings you erected at Scotia Bay as well as for the conveyance of our staff and materials to that place, and it gives me great pleasure to consider we may be able to carry on the scientific work so gloriously initiated and carried on under your direction during the past year. You have opened a new page in Nature's book of science, and I trust the legacy you have bequeathed to the Argentine Government will be cared for and studied, and the station be made permanent for the benefit of the world's meteorology and magnetism.*

The following day Bruce confirmed these proposed arrangements by writing to W H D Haggard in Buenos Aires, indicating that the decree issued by the British Consul, F D Harford, had been implemented and

> *… Robert Cockburn Mossman FRSE of Edinburgh, Meteorologist and Magnetist of the Scottish Expedition, will be asked to remain in charge of the observatory, and three scientific assistants of the Argentine Government will accompany the* Scotia *from Buenos Aires. William Smith of Dundee, second steward of the* Scotia, *at present with Mr. Mossman in the South Orkneys, will be asked to continue to act as cook and steward at Omond House. All these will be in the service of the Argentine Meteorological Office.*
>
> *I hand over to the Argentine Government the above building (Omond House), with a full supply of furniture and eighteen months' provisions, as well as the smaller wooden building for magnetism, viz: Copeland Observatory. I am landing such instruments as I can spare, which cannot be procured in the short time available to Mr. Davis.*

Thus Bruce introduced Argentina to a scientific station in Antarctica and it has remained in Argentine hands ever since, although in the early days several Scots, many of whom had served at Ben Nevis, were recruited to man the observatory. A list of all personnel is given in *Cuatro Anos en las Orcadas del Sur* (J M Moneta, Buenos Aires, 1954) for the years 1904-53, and until 1927 most of the staff were recruited from Western Europe. Of the three original Argentine scientists, Hugo Acuna was designated 'postmaster' and equipped with a cancellation stamp for the 'post office', Orcadas del Sud in Distrito 24 (Gallegos). This was the first post office in Antarctica, although it was *Scotia* that carried the first mail.

Subsequently Argentina claimed sovereignty over the South Orkney Islands by marking the sector from the South Pole to the Falkland Islands (Malvinas) which includes Laurie Island. Despite an invitation to both Chile and Argentina to have the question of the sovereignty of this part of Antarctica arbitrated at the International Court at the Hague in 1947 and 1955, neither country agreed to present its case. Today the South Orkney Islands are subject to the general measures of the Antarctic Treaty of 1962 and all territorial claims have been suspended *sine die*. Had he lived longer, Bruce would have been surprised and perhaps amused to see the geopolitical consequences of his actions, made in good faith and all in the name of science.

The Second Voyage to the Antarctic

Following her re-fit, *Scotia* sailed back to Laurie Island to land provisions and to pick up four of the party who had spent the summer there. Mossman and Smith remained until the following summer, seconded to the Argentinian Meteorological Service. The ship now sailed south and on 23 February 1904 headed for the eastern part of the Weddell Sea. It was Bruce's aim to reach as high a latitude as possible and by 3 March they were sailing through the ice-pack with an ice cliff visible from the crow's-nest to landward. Bruce correctly concluded that this was new land, but winter was closing in fast and the ship was in danger of becoming frozen into the pack.

He was right. On 7 March she was stuck solid 'like a fly in treacle' at 74°01'S 22°00'W, the furthest south the expedition would reach. Morale aboard *Scotia* fell; now there was a real possibility that the ship would be stuck all winter. As the weather brightened Bruce organised distractions for the scientists and crew such as football on the ice. Various quirky photographs were taken. One of these was of Gilbert Kerr, in full highland dress,

Above: Captain Thomas Robertson. (*SPRI*)

Left: Gilbert Kerr and penguin, off Coats Land, 10 March 1904. (*Glasgow University Archive*)

playing the pipes to an emperor penguin. As Harvey Pirie observed, 'neither rousing marches, lively reels, nor melancholy laments seemed to have any effect on these lethargic, phlegmatic birds'.

By the afternoon of 12 March, just as Bruce was beginning to think that it would be necessary to prepare for having to overwinter, the ice suddenly cracked and open water appeared near the ship. However, despite having all hands jump up and down on the ice at the same time, and even the use of explosives, they could not free *Scotia* – 'digging, hauling, shoving, jumping, running, blasting, were of no avail'.

At tea-time the following day Captain Robertson confided in Bruce that they were unlikely to escape the ice. But almost as he spoke the weather changed and the ice about the ship began to loosen. By six o'clock *Scotia* was able to make headway under steam.

Although they prepared to leave the ship in order to visit Coats Land, the state of the sea ice was such that Bruce abandoned the attempt rather than further imperil his ship and men. Instead he called for two bottles of champagne and handed round cigars to celebrate furthest south, and toasted sweethearts and wives and all supporters of the expedition. Bruce had reached almost as far south as James Weddell who, in a very favourable ice year, sailed to 74°15'S with the whalers *Jane* and *Beaufoy*. Not until 1911 was a higher southern latitude reached in this part of the Weddell Sea by the German army officer Filchner.

To honour his principal patrons, Bruce named the newly-discovered stretch of coastland Coats Land.

The heroes return. (RSGS)

[Ernest Shackleton's *Endurance,* sailing a similar course, was frozen solidly into the ice on 19 January 1915 in latitude 74° within sight of Coats Land. For *Endurance* there was to be no escape route. The ship was carried along in the ice by the Weddell Sea currents until it was crushed and sunk.]

Scotia now returned to Cape Town via Gough Island, and the daily programme of scientific measurements began again. Deep waters were dredged and trawled; sea temperatures and salinities measured; the direction of ocean currents recorded by throwing floats over the side; and meteorological readings taken by means of fixed instruments. On 23 March 1904, in the same area of sea where James Clark Ross recorded 4000 fathoms, 'no bottom', Bruce found glacial clay at 2660 fathoms and was able to correct the Admiralty Chart, deducing that the Antarctic coastline was closer than expected.

On her journey home, *Scotia* was anchored for four days in a bay in the remote sub-tropical Gough Island. There the scientists went ashore and Rudmose Brown was given a rare opportunity to indulge his passion for botanical collecting so singularly restricted in Antarctica.

They reached Cape Town on 6 May and *Scotia* sailed up the coast to

undertake a study of Suldanha Bay. On 24 May the ship left for the final leg of the voyage, calling only at St Helena and Ascension Islands before setting a course for the Clyde. Such good time was made on the journey home that *Scotia* reached the Irish Sea and anchored in Kingstown Harbour on 15 July. They were received warmly by the people of Kingstown, and also by the residents of Bangor and Larne as a preliminary taste of their welcome in Scotland.

Finally reaching the Clyde on 21 July 1904, the news of the success of the expedition had gone ahead of the ship and James Ferrier, secretary to the expedition, arranged a reception at the Marine Station, Millport. There was a great celebration as Scotland welcomed back its polar heroes. John Murray gave a speech of welcome, read a telegram of congratulations from the King, and presented Bruce with the Gold Medal of the Royal Scottish Geographical Society, and Captain Robertson with a silver medal. Both Bruce and Robertson replied to the welcome, before 400 guests sat down to luncheon.

The expedition had fulfilled all scientific expectations and brought back an extensive haul of eggs, skins and fishes and an assortment of rocks and other specimens, including seven new genera and more than 24 new species. In the three volumes of the post-voyage scientific reports dealing with invertebrates, a staggering total of 1100 species is recorded, of which 212 are described for the first time. In addition, hydrographic and topographic surveying had been carried out in areas known otherwise very sketchily, and a new outline of part of Antarctica had been discovered in Coats Land. Significantly, all officers and crew returned in good health, with the exception of the ill-fated Allan Ramsay.

Bruce was characteristically modest about the expedition's achievements, but was highly praised for his work by the scientific community. But national recognition of the success of the expedition was not forthcoming and neither Bruce nor any of his company were awarded the prestigious Polar Medal of the Royal Geographical Society, despite his continual protests. Those close to Bruce blamed Clements Markham for this failure.

And what became of *Scotia*? When Bruce returned from the Antarctic he would have preferred that Scotland adopted the ship as a training vessel for young seamen and naturalists, but the money was not forthcoming and Bruce was obliged to sell the ship in Dundee to meet the debts of the expedition. *Scotia* was re-fitted with new and larger engines as a whaler, and she sailed in 1905 under Captain Robertson bound for the Greenland Sea. In 1913, after the *Titanic* disaster, she was charted by the Board of Trade, again under Robertson, for the North Atlantic iceberg patrol and once more carried out scientific observations of ice and weather. The results were published in two volumes. Early in World War I the ship, acting as a collier, caught fire shortly after leaving Cardiff and ran aground. It burned out on the beach at Sully near Barry in the Bristol Channel (not, as reported by Rudmose Brown, in the Scilly Isles).

References

Bruce, William Speirs: *The Log of the* Scotia *Expedition, 1902-4* (editor, Peter Speak) (Edinburgh: Edinburgh University Press, 1992).
Reader's Digest: *Antarctica: Great Stories from the Frozen Continent* (Sydney, 1985).
Three of the Staff: *The Voyage of the Scotia* (Edinburgh, 1906).

CHAPTER 8

THE SCOTTISH
OCEANOGRAPHICAL LABORATORY

SHORTLY after the return from Antarctica, where Bruce had enjoyed excellent health in the germ-free atmosphere, he succumbed to a prolonged attack of influenza. Consequently the popular account of the expedition, *The Voyage of the Scotia,* was written by three of his colleagues. In deference to Bruce they wrote as 'Three of the Staff'. Bruce contributed only the Preface in which he included his stirring message to Scottish nationalists: 'While "Science" was the talisman of the Expedition, "Scotland" was emblazoned on its flag.'

Bruce was beginning to identify more and more with Scottish nationalism and regarding, with some justification, the Government and scientific institutions in London as hostile towards anything north of the Border. Burn Murdoch wrote of Bruce: 'Poor fellow, that was the bee in his bonnet and mine too, the belief in there being such a thing as Scottish Nationality.'

Bruce's focus of attention, however, had now turned to practicalities. Through his endeavours, both in the Arctic and Antarctic, he had amassed a very large collection of polar biological, zoological and geological specimens, as well as detailed records of scientific data. He now needed somewhere to store and display all these materials. A single storey building became available, adjacent to Surgeon's Hall in Nicolson Street, Edinburgh and it was here that Bruce housed his collections, catalogued the exhibits and stored his records. Notable among the specimens were a large sea lion (*Otaria jubata*), captured in the Falkland Islands, and a sunfish (*Mola mola*). With the co-operation of a few colleagues he assembled a unique oceanographical museum, maintained with the help of one assistant, R Turnbull.

The Scottish Oceanographical Laboratory was formally opened by His Serene Highness Prince Albert I of Monaco in 1906 at a ceremony attended by leading figures from Edinburgh's civic and academic communities. Bruce not only established the laboratory as the new headquarters of the Scottish National Antarctic Expedition for the preparation of the scientific reports, but made it his office and professional home. The oceanographic and meteorological apparatus from his Arctic and Antarctic voyages were also stored here, ready for the next venture, although they were always available

Scottish Oceanographical Laboratory – Bruce with his assistant Turnbull. (*Edinburgh University Library [EUL]*)

on loan to any worthy new expedition. From here Bruce corresponded vigorously with colleagues on interpretation of scientific data, with those preparing new expeditions, with the national press to correct ill-informed comments on matters where he felt he was an authority, and, when expedient, with politicians on the continent of Europe and in Australia and New Zealand. In turn Bruce sought advice from such eminent scholars as Sir Joseph Hooker, an aged survivor of the Erebus and Terror Antarctic Expedition of 1839-43. Bruce dedicated his little book entitled, *Polar Exploration* (1911), to Sir Joseph.

Although conveniently located in Edinburgh, the building was difficult to access and was exposed to the noxious preparations of a pickle factory in Drummond Street nearby. James Ferrier pointed out just how unpleasant it was, in a letter written to Bruce dated 19 January 1911:

> *I had a funny experience last night in the Lab. My stomach fairly turned through the stink of the pickle factory and I got round the corner barely in time. It was super-imposed double-action exhaust guff!*

Nonetheless Bruce entertained all his polar visitors here, explorers and scholars alike. Nansen and Amundsen visited; as did Shackleton who held the post of secretary to the Royal Scottish Geographical Society for a brief period in Edinburgh.

Bruce now faced the daunting prospect of compiling the *Scotia's* scientific reports. He was determined that the reports should be prepared by the highest authorities and sent his specimens and records to experts, a practice cultivated since his days in the Challenger office. He also attempted to employ only the very best engravers to illustrate the papers, using on several occasions A H Searle of the British Museum in London. Many of the scientific papers were first published in *Proceedings of the Royal Society of Edinburgh,* and then, by permission, incorporated into the *Scientific Results of the Scottish National Antarctic Expedition.* In this way some of the initial costs were avoided, or at least delayed.

As always Bruce was very short of money. The *Scotia* had been sold for £5000 in Dundee and had joined the whaling fleet in North Atlantic waters. Bruce still owed over £3000 from the expedition and estimated that he required a minimum of £6000 to publish the expedition's findings. He approached the Treasury for a grant of this sum, but failed at first to receive any support at all.

Bruce explained his financial predicament in a personal letter to Ferrier:

My Dear Mr. Ferrier
In reference to yours of yesterday's date, I am indebted to the following friends for personal help, i.e. to enable me to carry on the organisation of the 'Scotia' Expedition from the beginning, and to carry on editorial work and work connected with the handling of the collections since the return of the Expedition. The money has been advanced to me personally and privately, and is not acknowledged in the general accounts of the Expedition. I regard these sums as debts of honour, to be repaid when I have the opportunity to do so.

It is difficult to say how much I am personally out of pocket, but as you know I have put in my last penny in order to have the work carried on if possible to a successful issue. I may also say that by devoting myself to Polar Exploration since 1892 till 1909, during which time I have been on seven Arctic and two Antarctic Voyages, that I have placed myself in such a position to be out of the running for many Educational positions for which I have been fully trained.

I may add that most of my polar work has been done without remuneration.
Yours sincerely
Wm. S. Bruce

Bruce's reliance on the benevolence of his friends is all too evident. He had placed too much faith on the support he might obtain from scientific societies and from the Government, and his ongoing struggle to fund the reports inevitably led to considerable delays in their publication. The Log of the voyage, which he had written during the morning watches every day of the expedition, was virtually complete when *Scotia* came home and it was

Bruce (left), outside the Scottish Oceanographical Laboratory. *(EUL)*

initially proposed as the first volume of the scientific reports. Had he published this detailed account quickly, he might have excited popular interest in his work and found sufficient funds forthcoming to proceed with the rest of the reports. Bruce, however, always the man of science, gave priority to the more specialised reports. The Log itself was not prepared to printers' proof stage until 1913, and by then the money had run out; it was not finally published until 1992 after it was rediscovered.

With meticulous care, and after much delay, Bruce managed to write his own material and edit other scientists' contributions to the official reports of the expedition. They were entitled *Report on the Scientific Results of the Voyage of SY Scotia during the years 1902, 1903, and 1904, under the leadership of William S Bruce, LLD, FRSE*: volume I, prepared, but published only in 1992; volume II – *Physics*; volume III – *Botany*; volume IV – *Zoology*; volume V – *Zoology, Invertebrates*; volume VI – *Zoology, Invertebrates*; volume VII – *Zoology, Invertebrates*. Apart from volume I, the reports were published between 1907 and 1920, and other supplementary papers were published on glaciology, deep-sea deposits, physical oceanography and marine fossils at various times. The reports were produced in hardback format, with a handsome gilt-tooled cover illustrated with the Scottish Lion and the motto of the House of Stuart: *Nemo me impune lacessit* ('No one accuse me with impunity')!

Bruce always hoped that his Scottish Oceanographical Laboratory would become an embryonic foundation for a Scottish National Oceanographical Institute comparable to those of Prince Albert of Monaco in Monte Carlo and Paris. A meeting was held to discuss this proposal in the rooms of the Royal Society in Edinburgh on 26 May 1914. Professor James Geikie chaired the meeting and it was attended by some of the most influential of Scotland's scientists, including Professor Sir

A plate from the Scotia reports. (SPRI)

Edward Schäfer, Dr J G Bartholomew, Dr John Horne, Professor James Cossar Ewart and Dr Cargill Knott. Professor Geikie moved the proposal that the establishment of an oceanographical institute was desirable and that the deep-sea deposits gathered by John Murray, currently held in the Challenger office with the Challenger library, together with the 'very fine collection' of Arctic and Antarctic animals amassed by Bruce, could well form a permanent institute. The resolution was passed unanimously, an organising committee was formed under the presidency of Lord Strathclyde, but alas nothing came of it. [A British Oceanographical Institute was established much later in southern England, in Surrey.]

By 1919 Bruce had been unable to raise sufficient further funding for the laboratory, and the strain of almost single-handed administration was taking its toll. He was obliged to close down in 1919, dispersing his fine polar library to the University of Edinburgh, the maps and photographs to the Royal Scottish Geographical Society, and the collections and specimens to the Royal Scottish Museum (now the Royal Museum, part of the National Museums of Scotland).

In the same year he withdrew his nomination for a lectureship at the University of Aberdeen when he found out that his old friend Rudmose Brown was also a candidate for the position.

References

Bruce, William Speirs: *The Log of the* Scotia *Expedition, 1902-4* (editor, Peter Speak) (Edinburgh: Edinburgh University Press, 1992).
Rudmose Brown, Robert Neal: *A Naturalist at the Poles* (London, 1923).
Swinney, G N: 'Some new perspectives on the life of William Speirs Bruce (1867–1921), with a preliminary catalogue of the Bruce collection of manuscripts in the University of Edinburgh' in *Archives of Natural History,* vol 28, pp 285-311 (2001).

CHAPTER 9

THE SCOTTISH
SPITSBERGEN SYNDICATE

ABOUT his original visit to Spitsbergen with the Prince of Monaco in 1898, Bruce made the following observation:

> *I … visited Storfjord and landed on Barents Island and discovered oil shale there. I subsequently discovered coal at Advent Bay and gypsum at Sassen Bay and brought home samples of all three minerals.*

The deposits of coal and gypsum were there for all to see, outcropping in the cliffs around Storfjord. However, substantial and commercially exploitable quantities of oil were more elusive, perhaps even illusory, but were to haunt Bruce for the rest of his days. He believed that exploitable oil resources would prove to be a principal foundation for a mineral prospecting and mining company.

Bruce returned again to the archipelago with the Prince in 1899. At that time he visited Advent Bay and Sassen Bay again, as well as Coles Bay, Green Harbour and Bell Sound (Bellsund), turning north to survey Red Bay.

Later, in the summers of 1906 and 1907, Bruce found time to revisit Spitsbergen, although preoccupied by his work at the Scottish Oceanographical Laboratory. In 1906, at the invitation of the Prince of Monaco, Bruce became involved in the detailed topographic mapping of Prince Charles Foreland, the island off the western coast. Together with Ernest Miller, a young electrical engineer, and Gilbert Kerr, the piper from *Scotia*, they sailed to the island on board *Princesse Alice*. The men were set ashore on the uninhabited coast where they lived under canvas, until the ship collected them on its return to Norway. Rudmose Brown later commented, 'From his first visit Bruce retained a great affection for the Foreland and in the end came to regard it almost as his homeland. Unless it was the Scottish Highlands, there was no place he loved better.'

In 1907 Bruce returned to continue the topographical work, this time sailing in *Fønix* and accompanied by J Victor Burn Murdoch (cousin of William Gordon), Stewart Ross, Gilbert Kerr, and for part of the time Hjalmar Johansen, Nansen's companion on the *Fram*, and Gunnar Isachsen,

Scottish Spitsbergen Syndicate survey team taking a meal break:
John Mathieson, chief surveyor, in kilt. (RSGS)

captain of *Kvedfjord*. The map of Prince Charles Foreland was finally completed in 1909 with the help of John Mathieson, formerly with the Ordnance Survey.

On Prince Charles Foreland, Bruce found deposits of coal in tertiary measures, and some indication of iron ores. Based on his findings, he established a private mineral prospecting company, the Scottish Spitsbergen Syndicate, and a prospectus was issued in September of that year from the Scottish Oceanographical Laboratory under the names of William S Bruce and J Victor Burn Murdoch. The accountants were listed as Messrs Whitson and Methuen, 21 Rutland Street, Edinburgh.

It might seem incredible that any individual would venture capital to mine in such an inhospitable and remote environment. The Spitsbergen archipelago lies between 71° and 81°N and at that time was the most northerly part of the world to have permanent settlement. The nearest inhabited mainland coast, and therefore potential market, was Norway some 350 nautical miles away, although the early mining companies also considered markets along the Arctic coast of Russia as well as the possibility of exporting to Great Britain and North America.

There were, however, some geographical and geological advantages not immediately apparent. The west coast faces the Arctic Ocean, a northern extension of the North Atlantic, and benefits from the ameliorating effects of the south-westerly winds blowing across the relatively warm North

Atlantic Drift. This means that the harbours along the west coast can be expected, in most years, to remain ice-free for the four months from June to September. These harbours are deep fjords, glaciated inlets which penetrate well inland, and in the case of the two largest, Isforden and Bellsund, are the locations of the most accessible coal seams. Deep water alongside the quay can be guaranteed. Although the export of minerals would be seasonal, the mining could take place all year round, and the coal, gypsum, or iron ore stockpiled for the next summer season. As far as mining processes are concerned, the underground environment is the same all year, and the temperature in the mines constant, just below freezing, ideal for hard manual labour. Moreover, the permafrost ground does not require so much roof support as mines in warmer climates and the risk of gas pockets is considerably reduced. Bruce believed that miners would be prepared to seek employment in Spitsbergen and the production of minerals for an overseas market would be viable.

But the principal attraction to the entrepreneur was the legal state of Spitsbergen, as it was considered *terra nullius* by the international community. This implied that entitlement to a holding and the right to mine could be obtained by simply staking out a plot and registering this with the Government of your own country. There would be no land to purchase, no taxes to pay, and no harbour dues.

All these conditions were set out in the Syndicate's prospectus, 'For Private Circulation Only', sent to prominent businessmen in Edinburgh and Glasgow. The prospectus listed possible markets as Archangel, which had direct communication with Moscow; Norway, a country without coal deposits; and even Hudson's Bay, where empty grain trucks could utilise the Spitsbergen coal as a return cargo for the Prairies.

Bruce brought samples of the coal home and had them analysed by well-known firms of metallurgical chemists who reported that they were 'a very good steam coal' comparable to the Silkstone Seam in Great Britain.

Encouraged by the results, Bruce and Victor Burn Murdoch projected initially a nominal capital of £6000 in shares of ten pounds each, from which £3000 would be used for the 1909 expedition and £3000 allotted to the leaders of the expedition for their services. Bruce and Burn Murdoch would receive no payment other than their salaries. It was to be a mineral prospecting company, concerned primarily with coal, and not a mining company. The intention was ultimately to sell the mineral rights to a development company (when this was finally proposed in 1919, the plans came to nought). The prospectus outlined their objective: '… to equip an Expedition to proceed to Spitsbergen early in 1909 to secure at least two considerable areas known to the undersigned, and which last year were still not taken up, and such other areas as may be still available.'

The subscription list was drawn up, and at 4.15pm on 6 July 1909 Bruce sent the following telegram to Rudmose Brown in Aberdeen:

SYNDICATE FORMED, LEAVE IN ABOUT ONE WEEK. KEEP PRIVATE YET. BRUCE.

The original Syndicate was composed of friends: Dr Paul Rottenburg, a Glasgow merchant and lawyer who held shares valued at £300; Prince Albert of Monaco (£300); T Leslie Usher, an Edinburgh businessman and brother-in-law to William Gordon Burn Murdoch, who retained his interest for many years (£50); Sir John Murray (£200); and Robert Neal Rudmose Brown and John Mathieson who were to accompany Bruce on the 1909 and subsequent expeditions (£100 each). Charles Hanson Urmston, a company director, held shares at £50.

Bruce was the mainstay of the Syndicate; he had the vision of a successful commercial enterprise and possessed an unrivalled scientific knowledge gained through his previous visits to the islands. Until his death in 1921 he was in almost daily correspondence about Spitsbergen with the secretary of the Syndicate, Alfred Aitken, or Rudmose Brown, or the Foreign Office in London, or with the national press.

The first of the Syndicate's expeditions left Leith in 1909 in a chartered Granton trawler, *Conqueror*, under Captain F B Napier. The scientific staff aboard included Bruce and Rudmose Brown, the surveyor John Mathieson, the geologists Harry Hannay and Angus Peach, Alastair Geddes (the son of Patrick Geddes), Victor Burn Murdoch, and Gilbert Kerr. Bruce was in charge.

They visited Prince Charles Foreland first of all and the map, begun in 1906, was completed. The whole Foreland was annexed on behalf of the Syndicate. Then on the main island, Sassenbukta, near the head of Isforden, was explored and Bruce and Hannay made the long and arduous journey across Vest Spitsbergen from Isforden to Storfjorden and back to Tempelforden where further claim boards were set up. The Syndicate's claims to a very large part of Vest Spitsbergen were notified to the British Foreign Office on 27 January 1910; and in an Appendix, dated 12 August 1913, the whole of Barents Island, which Bruce had visited in 1898, was also claimed and a note to that effect was delivered to the British Legation in Kristiania (Oslo).

Hannay prepared a detailed geological and mineralogical report on the disposition of the coal and gypsum deposits and referred briefly to other mineral ores. Bruce was somewhat disappointed by the report, but accepted that 'Hannay is a cautious man'. Rudmose Brown, writing much later in 1920, commented that 'the expedition was most successful and opened the way for further work'.

Scottish Spitsbergen Syndicate survey team on Spitsbergen. (*RSGS*)

But the funds of the Syndicate were seriously depleted by the expedition. Only £4000 of the £6000 originally projected had been raised from subscribers, of which £3873 had already been spent by October 1909 (£2000 had gone to Bruce and Burn Murdoch, £1845 was spent on the expedition, and the rest used up in general expenses). Until more capital could be raised, any further expeditions would have to be of a modest nature.

In 1912 Bruce and Rudmose Brown sailed on the Norwegian postal vessel *Dion* and inspected lands in Sassen Bay, Bjona Haven, and in the Gips Valley. They returned aboard *William Munroe* to Edinburgh on 6 September 1912 and filed a detailed report with the Syndicate in which they noted increased activities by Norwegian and Russian prospectors and the success of the American mine at Longyearbyen. Bruce added: 'One Power, and a strong one, must control the destinies of Spitsbergen. The one that is best able to do it and has fully as much claim as any other is Britain.' Already in 1912 the Northern Powers were meeting in Kristiania to discuss the future of Spitsbergen.

Another small expedition was planned for 1914. It comprised Bruce, Burn Murdoch, R M Craig, a geologist from the University of St Andrews, and John H Koeppern, a Scottish zoologist of German extraction who changed his surname by the end of the war to Kenneth. They intended to survey the head of Storfjorden and to search for the oil shale on Barents Island that Bruce had collected a sample of in 1898.

They charted the 46-ton vessel *Pelikane* for the journey, but found exceptionally severe ice conditions in Storfjorden. They only learned about

the outbreak of war on the mainland of Europe when they reached Gronfjorden on 12 August. Bruce wanted to return immediately but he was obliged, in order to defray expenses, to deliver his small cargo of fish and paraffin to the Russians and coal to the Germans at Ebeltoft. This done, and with little new exploration achieved, the ship headed back for Edinburgh to await developments.

The Syndicate was not the only company with the commercial vision to exploit the natural resources of Spitsbergen during the first two decades of the twentieth century. The most successful was the Arctic Coal Company of Boston. Founded in 1905 by two American entrepreneurs, John Longyear and Frederick Ayer, the company mined coal in Advent Bay close to what has become the principal settlement and centre of administration, Long-yearbyen (Longyear City). Longyear and Ayer were rich businessmen and international speculators. They had bought out the mining options of the Trondhjem Kulkompagnie in the extensive tertiary coalfields of Advent Bay and chartered their own company on 8 February 1906 in West Virginia. It was registered with the United States Secretary of State, Elihu Root, on 1 March 1906. With an initial capital of $100,000 (compared with the Syndicate's £4000), it was producing coal at an annual rate of 40,000 tonnes by 1914. When it became expedient they did not hesitate to sell to the Norwegian state enterprise, Store Norske Spitsbergen Kulkompagni Aktieselskap of Kristiania (Oslo), the company which is still mining some coal today at Longyearbyen and Sveagruva. There were, however, other companies registered over the years as either exploration or mining concerns:

Registered Companies (Exploration or Mining):

Year	Company
1905	Arctic Coal Co of Boston
1905	Spitsbergen Coal and Trading Co of Sheffield
1905	Spitsbergen Mining and Exploration Co (owned by E Mansfield and Rev. FT Gardner)
1906	Northern Exploration Co of London (for marble, King's Bay, 1910)
1909	Scottish Spitsbergen Syndicate (took over Mansfield and Gardner, 1905, and the Earl of Morton, 1906)
1910	Svenska Stenkole Spitsbergen A/B of Stockholm
1910	Anglo-Russian Grumant Co of London
1912	Russiske Kulfelter, registered in St Petersburg as M Levin & Co, but ostensibly Norwegian
1916	Norske Kulfelter A/S of Bergen take over Spitsbergen Coal and Trading Co
1916	King's Bay Kul Kompagni A/S take up claims made originally in 1901 by Bergen A/S
1916	Svalbard Kulgrubber A/S owned by Adolf Hoel and Staxrud, later Adventalens Kulfelter A/S, but never worked
1916	Store Norske Spitsbergen Kulkompagni A/S purchase the estates of Longyear and Ayer
1918	Northern Exploration Co revived by F Salisbury Jones (an abortive expedition under Ernest Shackleton)
1920	Nederlandsche Spitsbergen Co bought estates of Russiske Kulfelter. Sold to Soviet Arktik Ugol in 1932 who acquired Anglo-Russian Grumant Co
1932	Store Norske bought out Northern Exploration Co and the Sveagruva mine of Svenska Stenkole

Of these companies some were too small to be effective and the outbreak of World War I interrupted further prospecting. Only Store Norske and the Russian Arctic Ugol mining at Barentsburg and Pyramiden have survived to the present time. Yet of them all the Scottish Spitsbergen Syndicate had the largest registered holdings with 2980 square miles (7718 square km) by 1920.

Other businesses registered in London included the Spitsbergen Mining and Exploration Company with a nominal capital of £15,350 and 82 shareholders, the Spitsbergen Coal and Trading Company of Sheffield with £25,000 and 102 shareholders by 1908, and Spitsbergen United of London with a nominal capital of £10,000 and two directors (E B White, a dental surgeon, and A G Wedmore, an inspector of schools). Hence the only serious rival to Bruce's company in the United Kingdom was the Northern Exploration Company, with a capital issue increased to £100,000 in October 1912. It offered shares to the general public in 1918, much to the consternation of the Edinburgh-based Syndicate. Rudmose Brown noted:

> The NEC [Northern Exploration Company] *are launching pamphlets etc. on the City. Of course they contain bluff and some lies but whatever we do we must not*

contradict them. That would spoil any chance of the boom helping us ... we ought to get a paragraph in the Press that another company is also operating in Spitsbergen, namely S.S.S.

And in similar vein Burn Murdoch wrote to another shareholder: 'Assume if you like that all the NEC people are rogues. I don't see that they can hurt us very much if our Board is wide awake. That they should try and get a dry option on our claims (on dirt terms) is natural enough, and no crime.'

It was not just the actions of rival companies that the Syndicate needed to watch out for, but the underlying issue of the status of *terra nullius* in the islands, as this determined the financial advantage of investing in a remote and harsh environment. Countries like Norway, Sweden, Russia, the United Kingdom and United States of America were becoming increasingly interested in the issue of sovereignty. Although Norway's case, based on geographical proximity, appeared strong, Norway had shown very little interest in the archipelago until it achieved its independence from Sweden in 1905. It had been part of a Union with Sweden since 1814 when it broke its 500-year association with Denmark. However in 1905 the Prince of Denmark became King Haakon VII of Norway and the fate of the northern islands became a more significant issue.

The discovery of Spitsbergen is usually ascribed to the Dutch whaler William Barents in 1596 and registered with the States General of the Netherlands, but in 1614 the Muscovy Company of London, on a whaling expedition, claimed the island group for Great Britain, setting up a notice with the arms of King James I in Magdalena Bay and bringing back rocks and earth to deposit in the King's court. The Dutch were informed of this claim and a dispute continued for some time between the two countries until the middle of the seventeenth century when whaling declined, the whaling fleets moved further west, and the international community lost interest in Spitsbergen. In 1871, following Nordenskjöld's crossing of the main island in 1864, a proposal for the establishment of a joint Nor-wegian-Swedish scientific community came to nothing, the Powers prefer-ring that *terra nullius* should continue. In 1907 Norway again approached these countries and America, indicating that some form of internal control was essential and complete *laissez faire* was dangerous for the security of the mines and the miners. Sir Edward Grey at the British Foreign Office, and the Americans, preferred a neutral situation. The mine manager of the Arctic Coal Company, F P Burrall, stated on 31 October 1909:

The proposed Spitsbergen Conference has been called by Norway ... and unless a strong effort is made to the contrary, Norwegian interests will dominate all others .... Norway's plan is to have the administration of the Government of the islands left

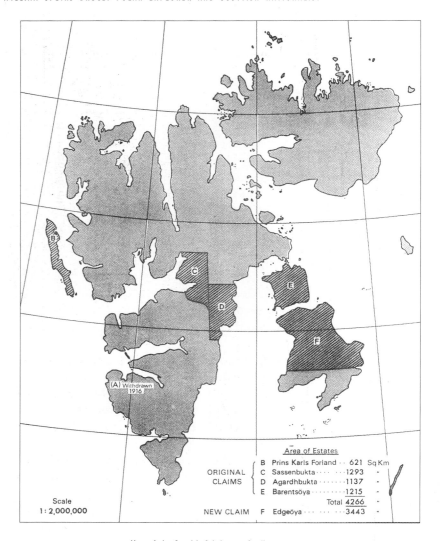

Map of the Scottish Spitsbergen Syndicate estates.

entirely to it, applying without restriction the Norwegian laws in both criminal and civil cases.

Conferences on the future of Spitsbergen were called by Norway in Kristiania in 1910 and 1912, attended by the three northern powers, and again in 1914 when all countries of north-west Europe, including the United Kingdom, were represented, as well as America. No changes were agreed and the questions of sovereignty, taxation and administration were put on hold until the end of the war.

Commercial mining in Spitsbergen. (RSGS)

From 1912–19 the question of the sovereignty of Spitsbergen exercised Bruce's mind unduly, as he could see the advantages of the archipelago being taken over by a sovereign state. It would give security of tenure to foreign firms working there, it would provide a police force to keep order and give aid to anyone in distress, as well as create a legal system to adjudicate on acts of disorder. He firmly believed that the Sovereign Power should be the United Kingdom and he invoked the 1614 Declaration as justification. Whether the United Kingdom had a genuine case under International Law was a matter for debate.

He wrote to his colleagues, to Edinburgh-based members of parliament, to the national press, and addressed professional bodies about the matter. In all, 50 letters were exchanged between the Syndicate and the Foreign Office. The following was sent to Bruce's constituency MP for Edinburgh from Winston S Churchill, the First Lord of the Admiralty, on 11 October 1912:

I am very much obliged to you for sending me Dr. Bruce's letter which I return. I have had the matter carefully considered by my expert advisors, and they have shown me good reason for thinking that it would be useless for us to assert a claim to Spitsbergen if it were possible to do so.

However, Bruce did find some allies in Whitehall, notably Admiral Parry, who wrote to him in 1916:

Unfortunately at present, the Foreign Office seem averse to the permanent acquisition of the really valuable 'No-Man's Land'; it is absolutely certain if we do not take action now, that in future years our descendants will heartily curse our slackness [and] I fear that the Foreign Office are not alive to the enormously important position of Spitsbergen either economically or strategically.

But in 1917 Churchill wrote to Milne Henderson in Edinburgh:

There are no naval reasons which would make the annexation of the island by this country necessary at the present time, particularly as a purely formal annexation without the presence of an armed force would not in itself affect whatever possibility may exist of the island being used by our enemies.

In August 1918 the Syndicate secretary, Alfred Aitken, commented to Rudmose Brown: 'I cannot fathom the malign influence that seems to dog our Leader in his efforts at the Foreign Office, and possibly the Admiralty also. I used to think it was Markham but the influence still seems to be there.'

But perhaps it was simply not the time to pursue such matters: the world was still reeling from the effects of the Great War and Spitsbergen's sovereignty was an issue that was easy to defer until later. As Prime Minister A J Balfour observed: 'The present moment is not opportune for bringing forward matters of this nature.'

In late 1918 Sir Ronald Graham of the Foreign Office gave an interview to Bruce and Marples (secretary, Northern Exploration Company) suggesting that a diplomatic 'quid-pro-quo solution' was likely to the Spitsbergen question:

Denmark was likely to be given control of Schleswig, Sweden was likely to be given control of the Baltic Islands, and Norway would likely want control of Spitsbergen, that Britain had great interests in the East, in Mesopotamia and elsewhere, that France had similar interests in Africa.

It was clear that HM Government was not prepared to make an issue over this northern outpost for the sake of a few mining companies whose total output thus far was negligible; and although Spitsbergen was seen to be advantageous as a location for a wireless and meteorological station, the further strategic situation of the archipelago at the entrance to the Northern Seaway along the coast eastwards to the Bering Straits had not yet been contemplated.

It was convenient to convene a conference on Spitsbergen whilst the major Powers were assembled in Paris for the Versailles Treaty Agreement to conclude the war. The Spitsbergen Treaty was signed in Paris on 9 February 1920 by the representatives of the High Contracting Parties: the United States of America, United Kingdom, Denmark, France, Italy, Japan, Norway,

Netherlands and Sweden. Germany, as the defeated nation, was not a signatory; neither was Russia because of the general non-recognition of the new communist regime, but informal assurances were given by Russia to Norway on 13 February 1924 of her unconditional recognition of Norway's sovereignty over the archipelago. Ratification of the Treaty did not take place until 1925 and on 14 August of that year the Norwegian flag was unfurled over Longyearbyen at an official ceremony and Spitsbergen became part of the kingdom of Norway. America failed to recognise the Government of the Soviet Union until 1933 and so the official adherence of the Central Executive of the Union of Soviet Socialist Republics was delayed until 27 February 1935 and came into effect on 7 May 1935. Thereafter Russia became an important exploiter of coal establishing a large coal mine with a settlement to rival Longyearbyen at Barentsburg and a smaller mine at Pyramiden.

The terms of the Spitsbergen Treaty attempted to safeguard the existing claims to mineral exploitation and mining by a 'favoured nation' clause:

ARTICLE 3: *The nationals of all the High Contracting Parties shall have equal liberty of access and entry for any reason or object whatsoever to the waters, fjords and ports of the territories specified; subject to the observance of local laws and regulations, they may carry on there without impediment all marine, industrial, mining and commercial operations on a footing of absolute equality.*

It appeared that, despite the delay, the lobbying done by Bruce and others had resulted in some important advantages for those nationals of the signatory countries who had economic development in mind. Although the Treaty gave Norway the responsibility for keeping law and order, there was a clause (ARTICLE 9) prohibiting the development of any kind of military installations. Hunting rights would be reserved exclusively for the benefit of occupiers of land within 6.2 miles (9.9km) of their headquarters (ARTICLE 2), and 'taxes, duties and dues shall be devoted exclusively to the said territories, and shall not exceed what is required for the object in view' (ARTICLE 8), continuing: 'so far, particularly as the exportation of minerals is concerned the Norwegian Government shall have the right to levy an export duty which shall not exceed 1% of the maximum value of the minerals exported up to 100,000 tons, and beyond that quantity the duty will be proportionately diminished.'

These clauses were by no means restrictive and companies with legitimate claims and serious purpose continued their work in the area. The Scottish Spitsbergen Syndicate began to prepare a case for exploitation by instructing its solicitors, Messrs Hagart of Edinburgh, to deal with the Foreign Office in London, who in turn corresponded with the commissioner specially appointed to examine all possible claimants.

In 1920 the High Contracting Parties agreed that mining regulations should be prepared and they appointed a neutral adjudicator for the purpose, a Dane, Dr Kristian Sindballe. The Mining Ordinance for Spitsbergen was promulgated on 7 August 1925 and published as an Annexe to the Treaty. It stated that within three months of the Treaty coming into force any Government whose nationals had claims prior to the signature of the Treaty should notify the commissioner of those claims, delimiting them on a map, scale no less than 1:1,000,000, and pay one penny per acre of land claimed to defray the expenses of the examination. A lawyer representing the Syndicate, A Mathew, in an address before the commissioner in Oslo on 4 February 1925, stated that 'in 1919 the total area claimed by us amounted to 2980 square miles, but we have now restricted our total claim in Spitsbergen to 100 square miles'.

This was a substantial reduction from the original claims by Bruce, but as Mathew pointed out the Syndicate had spent about £150,000 between 1909 and 1925 on its many expeditions. Accordingly, he deposited £305.13s.4d. at the rate of one penny per acre with the commissioner. In truth this was now almost the entire money left in the Syndicate's funds. Since 1909 they had neither mined nor exported coal or any other mineral.

In order to establish the serious intent of any claimant, it was further stated in the Mining Ordinance that mining operations should begin, and in any successive period of five years that at least '1,500 man-days work' should be employed. However, for companies like the Scottish Spitsbergen Syndicate with acts of appropriation before the signing of the Treaty, a period of ten years could elapse before mining operations should be demonstrated. Otherwise the claim would be deemed to have lapsed.

Back in 1918 Bruce and Burn Murdoch were beginning to lack confidence in the Syndicate's business acumen, although its scientific expertise was not in question. Bruce wrote to Rudmose Brown in that year:

> It will probably be wise for me to resign Chairmanship of Directors if we can get a man like Leslie Usher to replace me as a prominent Glasgow businessman. I strongly believe in the Glasgow element rather than the Edinburgh element managing the business for us. I am not a businessman myself.

Once the war was over the Syndicate's hopes had been encouraged by the prospect of a revival of international trade. But the funds of the company were seriously depleted and Bruce realised they only had three options: sell the assets to another company, effect a merger with another company, or turn to the British public for more funds. All three options were explored and eventually Bruce persuaded the Syndicate to enlarge by a public issue of shares on the London Stock Exchange. An extra-ordinary meeting was held in Edinburgh on 16 January 1919 where it was agreed to wind up the existing company, and to replace it with a new company with a nominal capital of £100,000 and an issue of 85,000 shares at £1 each. The new directors were almost all businessmen this time, with the exception of William Gordon Burn Murdoch: J Maxton Graham (chairman), J B Bolton, H M Cadell, Charles Hanson Urmston and T Leslie Usher. Bruce stood down as a director.

The aims of the new Syndicate were ambitious and all-embracing. In its Memorandum and Articles it stated its purpose:

- *To acquire by concession, purchase, lease, or otherwise, and possess or obtain, exploit, work and develop lands and estates and rights, interests, options and privileges, in land, gold, silver, platinum, copper, iron, coal, lime, gypsum, oil, etc.*
- *To carry on in Spitsbergen or elsewhere, the business of whaling, fishing, pursuing, killing and dealing, in fish, game, skins, and manufactures, fur dealers, trawl owners, ship owners, hotel keepers, brewers, etc;*
- *To purchase, build, acquire, charter, or otherwise provide ships, boats, plant, instruments, appliances, etc.*

In addition, the Syndicate planned to erect buildings, factories, furnaces and wireless stations, and to construct reservoirs, build roads and harbours, *etc.* Nothing that was likely to bring commercial gain was omitted.

With the new capital a major expedition was undertaken in the summer of 1919 with Bruce in charge and Rudmose Brown as his deputy. There was an impressive scientific and mining staff drawn principally from the universities in Scotland. These included Victor Burn Murdoch, A F Campbell, G W Tyrell, J M Wordie, J K M Charlesworth, Douglas A Allan, G Ross, C M Leitch, C Raeburn, J Stevens, W R Dron (a professor of mining from Glasgow), H Sandys (geologists), John Mathieson, G M Cowan (surveyors), C M Scott (secretary), and Robley Browne (medical officer). Bruce and Rudmose Brown received £600 and £500 respectively for their services, and the rest smaller sums.

All the estates claimed by the Syndicate were visited, two houses erected and trial mining begun. The scientific specialists looked upon this as a new and rewarding experience carried out in the long university vacation and produced detailed reports on returning to Scotland. Charlesworth and Stevens later became professors of geology; and Wordie, who had accompanied Ernest Shackleton to the Antarctic on *Endurance*, became master of St John's College, Cambridge, and chairman of the committee of management of the Scott Polar Research Institute. None of the other Spitsbergen companies was better advised as far as scientific matters were concerned.

Although no precious mineral deposits were discovered, Bruce still believed in the presence of oil shale, or even free oil, and wrote to Rudmose Brown on 19 February 1919: 'If you meet [Hannay], get him to describe, as detailed as possible, where he and I alone smelt Broxburn. Personally I greatly believe in this spot and I could easily find it, if carried there, failing my walking powers. It was a remarkable smell! Reeking, real reeking!'

The spot was examined by Wordie, Tyrell and Cowan around the foot of the Usher Glacier near Mohn Bay, where a strong bituminous smell arose from a gorge in a swift glacial river. Wordie and Tyrell agreed that 'the smell of natural gas is strong in the gorge and in the ice-cave'. Tyrell believed it was caused by 'the liberation of gas from bituminous rocks by the trituration of wave-rolled fragments, but is more likely to be due to natural gas escaping from small faults and fissures'. But no occurrence of free oil was found in the Storfjorden area and Stevens concluded there were no structures favourable for oil in the area. Bruce's long-cherished hopes for the discovery of oil were beginning to fade.

Bruce's health was already failing in 1919 and the following year he went on the Syndicate's expedition as an adviser rather than a full member. The 1920 expedition of fifty scientists and members was led by surveyor John Mathieson who continued to lead expeditions until 1928. Many of the 1919 scientists went again in 1920 and Wordie and Tyrell finally resolved the oil question: 'There are no signs of free oil, and the geological structure is extremely unfavourable for the accumulation of that mineral,' they stated in their joint report. Wordie, in a separate report to Mathieson, added: 'On the properties at present held by the Syndicate I do not think free oil will ever be found.' (More recent detailed surveys for oil carried out in this area and on Barents Island have been no more encouraging.) Mathieson recommended that the Syndicate should concentrate its attention on the potential of the coalfields in the Klaas Billen and Gips Valley areas.

The 1921 expedition was much smaller, ten members in all, including the return of Professor W R Dron who had been with the 1919 group. Bruce was too ill to accompany them and Rudmose Brown took on the role of chief advisor to this and all subsequent expeditions. These were reconnaissance expeditions led by Mathieson, plus two or three other scientists.

Funds were now very low; the expeditions from 1919 to 1928 cost £9269 and the cash balance available to the company at the end of 1929 was only £154. The post-war economic boom was also over, the price of coal and other minerals had fallen heavily on the world markets, and Spitsbergen lost its attraction to speculators. Apart from the small amount of cash, all the company had left were the Spitsbergen assets, the potential of the claims, and some mining equipment.

After World War II the company's claims were re-examined by Group Captain C W E Urmston, who had inherited shares from his uncle, Charles Hanson Urmston, and William Gordon Burn Murdoch, his cousin, both directors of the Syndicate on its formation in 1909. Captain Urmston visited the Syndicate properties in Spitsbergen in 1948 and commissioned a technical report from Powell Duffryn, the mining and metallurgical group of South Wales, who reported in 1951 on the difficulties of developing the area at that time and estimated that the total capital cost would be £1,862,000. There was no possibility of raising money of this magnitude. Moreover the Syndicate had accepted an offer in 1950 from Captain Urmston of £5000 for the capital assets of the company plus a five per cent interest in any profit that might be made. On 7 June 1952 the Norwegian Government agreed to buy the estates and all claims for the sum of £27,500 and the properties and claims were taken over by Store Norske, the Longyear-based coal company. The official British liquidator on 22 June 1953 issued the following notice to all shareholders of Urmston's company: 'Notice is hereby given that a first and final distribution of assets at the rate of 0.8784 pence per share has been declared.'

Rudmose Brown, who had become a director of the company in 1941, and who had retired from his post as professor of geography at the University of Sheffield, possessed 680 Founders' Shares and received a cheque for £2.9s.9d. This was the end of the Scottish Spitsbergen Syndicate.

The academics recruited by the Syndicate had spent several long summer vacations in an exciting northern environment, and the businessmen had lost only small amounts in a highly speculative venture. Had he lived, however, William Speirs Bruce would have taken this outcome rather more grievously.

The coal mines operated by the Norwegian and Russian companies were still being exploited in the 1990s, although in recent years the numbers working there have been in decline. In 1995 the total production from Store Norske Spitsbergen Kulkompagni was around 300,000 tons from mines in the area around Longyearbyen and Sveagruva, with 280 employees; the Russian mines at Barentsburg and Pyramiden produced some 500,000 tons, supporting a population of about 1700.

References

Hisdal, V: *Svalbard – Nature and History* (Oslo, 1998).
Mathisen, T: *Svalbard in International Politics* (Oslo, 1954).
Mathisen, T: *Svalbard in the Changing Arctic* (Oslo, 1954).
Østreng W: *Politics in High Latitudes* (London, 1977).
Rudmose Brown, Robert Neal: *Spitsbergen* (London, 1920).
Singh, E C: 'The Spitsbergen (Svalbard) Question', United States Foreign Policy, 1907–1935 (Oslo, 1980).
Unstein, G: *Svalbard Treaty* (Oslo, 1995).
Umbreit, A: *Guide to Spitsbergen* (Chalfont St Peter, 1991).

CHAPTER 10

FINAL ENDEAVOURS

The New Scottish Antarctic Expedition

AFTER the return of *Scotia* in 1904, Bruce was heavily occupied with expedition reports, the Scottish Oceanographical Laboratory, visiting Spitsbergen and founding the Syndicate. He had little time for another expedition south, but followed with interest the fortunes of others in their scientific enquiries and search for the Pole, corresponding in particular with Captain Scott, Jean-Baptiste Charcot and Ernest Shackleton.

However, Bruce was growing anxious to lead another Antarctic expedition himself, but this time to include an attempt at the coveted prize of first at the Pole. It was a major change in his attitude. For Bruce, science had always been the prime objective. The man of science 'opens the way, and reveals the treasures of the unknown, and the man of business follows and reaps the commercial advantage'. Now, perhaps too late, he was beginning to realise that the public also demanded heroes of their explorers. They must overcome adversity and face danger with equanimity in order to place the British flag over new territorial gains.

As the years passed he became acutely aware of the value to potential sponsors of being the first to reach the Pole, and of course, in Bruce's mind, it would be a major achievement for Scotland as a nation. Nonetheless, he still insisted that it would not be at the expense of the scientific opportunities en route. There was a considerable amount of oceanographic work still to be done in the Weddell and Ross Seas.

Bruce began to develop a proposal for a second Scottish Antarctic expedition, one which would cross Antarctica via the Pole. He wrote to Mill on 3 March 1910, asking for his support:

> *I am desired by the Council of the Royal Scottish Geographical Society to ask you if you could attend a meeting of the Society on the evening of March 17 which has for its object the promotion of the new Scottish Antarctic Expedition, and to ask if you would say a few words in support of the project on that occasion. The arrange-ment is that I give them an outline of the plans with lantern illustrations and that about half a dozen speakers who are authorities on the subject speak in support. Your special association with the history of Antarctic Exploration and the fact that*

you were the first one to support me in Antarctic research is the special reason of asking you to do this. I enclose an outline of the plans, which include reaching the South Pole, because they include crossing Antarctica from Atlantic to Pacific. Anything, however, in the nature of a Marathon race is not included in the programme.

But by this time Captain Scott was already well advanced with his plans for a British assault on the South Pole. Bruce wrote to him aboard *Terra Nova* on 15 October 1911:

Yesterday's papers announce the arrival of the Terra Nova *at Melbourne so I hasten to send you a line in the first place to wish you complete success in every respect, and in the second to attempt to answer some of your friendly criticisms of my plans in your letter of September 28 and 29th of last year, which owing to an inability to meet each other we were unable to fully discuss.*

In the first place if you read my remarks again you will find that you have misread what I have stated. I have never intended to get up a station at McMurdo Sound but only to have my ship there for say two or three months during the second summer of the expedition, and since the ship will only be here for purposes of relief, I don't think there should be any clashing with another expedition stationed in a house there. Another point is that I have my ship going to Coats Land only during the first season and concentrate my whole energy in setting up the fully equipped wintering station there. It would be a quite impossible arrangement to be at McMurdo Sound till Jan. 15th and hammer it out to Coats Land with ponies, dogs and arrive there if at all when the summer season was done, viz. the middle of March.

I enclose again a copy of the printed plans published by the [Royal Scottish Geographical Society], *and you will see it is as briefly as follows:*

1st summer. Ship goes direct from Cape Town to Coats Land or to eastward and having set up station proceeds to Melbourne.

2nd summer. Ship goes from Melbourne or Port Lyttleton to McMurdo Sound with relief party and supplies. Ship stands by while relief party pushes south to meet party set out from Coats Land this same season and returns to Port Lyttleton or suitable port in New Zealand or Australia with the Trans-Continental Party on board, and then proceeds to say, Puntas Arenas or Falklands.

3rd summer. Ship pushes south to Coats Land Station and takes the remaining members of the wintering station home.

Extensive oceanographical research forms the chief feature of the expedition.

The expedition cannot leave Britain before 1912 because funds are not yet sufficient owing to action of His Majesty's Treasury refusing a grant for the work up to this date. So perhaps you will be getting back when I am setting out.

Whatever happens however I wish you good luck and hope you will settle up the South Pole. You are sure to bring back a rich harvest of scientific results which cannot fail to be of the deepest interest and importance, and no one will be keener than myself to hear your story on your return. Good luck and au revoir. I only wish we could have had a talk.

This outline to Scott was precisely the same as the one agreed at a meeting held in Edinburgh on 17 March 1910, addressed by Bruce, and chaired by the President of the Royal Scottish Geographical Society, Professor James Geikie. It was printed in the Society's journal for 1910 under the title 'The New Scottish National Antarctic Expedition 1911' and given the support of the Society. Others pledged support on behalf of sister organisations: Dr John Horne for the Royal Society of Edinburgh; Professor Graham Kerr for the Royal Philosophical Society of Glasgow; the Earl of Cassilis for the St Andrew Society; Professor Cossar Ewart for the University of Edinburgh; Professor D'Arcy Thompson for the Scottish Fishery Board and Dundee University College; George Chisholm for Scottish Geographers; and Rudmose Brown for the *Scotia* scientists who knew Bruce well.

The expedition was originally planned to leave around 1 May 1911 in order to reach Buenos Aires about 20 June. The total cost would be *circa* £50,000. However, in spite of the new wave of enthusiasm for another Scottish Antarctic expedition, no rich benefactor came forward in Scotland and Bruce failed to persuade any Government department in London to pledge funds. Moreover, the timing seemed unpropitious for yet another expedition at this particular point of the Heroic Age; Shackleton was talking about an Imperial Trans-Antarctic Expedition following a route very similar to that proposed by Bruce; and Scott, with Government backing, public money and the blessing of the London societies, was organising the *Terra Nova* Expedition with the express aim of attempting the South Pole.

Undeterred by any thought of competition, and secure in the professional friendship of his rivals, Bruce lobbied all Scottish members of parliament to approach the Prime Minister, the Treasury and the Admiralty for a favourable outcome. With hindsight it seemed certain that in the minds of members and ministers there was confusion about Bruce's requests, for the question of a grant for the publication of the Scotia reports had not yet been settled, and for many the prospect of grants for two Scottish Antarctic expeditions was anathema.

Bruce wrote to Mill from Edinburgh on 19 March 1910:

... I wish I had known of your power in the direction you mention. The full notice that an appeal was being made appeared in the papers at the end of November and I thought everybody knew about it. It created a great stir in Scotland, but of course London does not care a rap about us in the North. However we shall all be glad if you will do what you can. I suppose one of the Members of Parliament who has tackled you is Mr. Price who has been taking the leading part in the business.

He had told me that he has written to different members of the Deputation. I am sure your notes will be of greatest possible use.

Charles E Price was Bruce's constituency MP who had worked hard in the corridors of the House of Commons on his behalf, raising the matter of grants for both the Scotia and the proposed new Scottish expeditions to the Antarctic. He wrote to Bruce on 4 March 1910 suggesting that the request was too modest: 'You should have asked for £10,000 as one rarely gets all one asks for.'

Throughout March, Price tried to organise a deputation to the Chancellor of the Exchequer led by the Lord Advocate, and the Master of Elibank agreed to try to see Lloyd George, the Prime Minister – but neither were available. Bruce was frustrated by the Government's continuing procrastination on both matters, but the Treasury eventually wrote to offer a grant of £3000 towards the costs of publication of the scientific results of the Scotia Expedition (Bruce had requested £6800). Lloyd George suggested that the remainder of Bruce's requested funding should be raised in Scotland, in spite of his knowledge that the whole of the initial cost of the 1902-04 Scottish National Antarctic Expedition had been raised by Scottish benefactors and subscribers, and that the published scientific results would have international circulation. Notwithstanding these setbacks, Bruce continued to make further applications to the British Government until 1915.

His loyal friend, James Ferrier, wrote to Bruce in September 1910:

… You will see that as regards the Treasury you are much as you were, indeed the last clause of the letter leaves you worse to my mind. Another volume cannot be brought out in a week or a month, and you won't get a penny until one is out. Meanwhile that awful pile of overdue accounts is frightful to think about. I am truly sorry that this should meet you first thing on your return from Switzerland, for you had little need of discouragement.

Not all the Scottish members, however, were loyal to the cause, as Ferrier disclosed in a letter dated 25 November 1910:

I have just had a conversation with Price who has seen both Elibank and the Chancellor. He left Macallister's letter with Lloyd George who was, at the moment, too busy to deal with it, but Price was sure it would have a good effect, 'as only the restrictions of the grant had to be removed'. He is quite at one with a protest by the 'St. Andrew's Society'. He is very indignant, and styled the conduct of certain Scottish members who have been working against a grant from the beginning. 'If we could get their names what a mess we could make of them at this time. They ought to be exposed.'

And the following day he writes yet again:'This is a hopeless day to get near Lloyd George, and Whitson will have nothing to do with it. Personally I think Price will do all that is necessary, and Elibank is pledged to see it through.'

Rudmose Brown, in rough notebook jottings, summarised the position over the grants at this time:

> Government gave Captain Scott for expeditions up to 1909 (Discovery), £99000.
> Government gave Scott for Terra Nova in 1910, £20000.
> Government gave Shackleton in August 1909, £20000.
> Government gave Shackleton, March 1914, for Endurance, £10000.

The Scotia Expedition, on the other hand, which had by 1914 (with the publications, etc) cost £40,000, received only £3000, agreed by Lloyd George in May 1910 but not released until a year later. By this time, when all liabilities had been paid, Bruce was left with only £800 for any new venture.

Bruce expressed his delight at the support given to both Scott and to Shackleton, but could not accept the lack of enthusiasm in London for a complementary expedition originating in Scotland. With his nationalistic obsession, and his characteristic naïveté in matters of political diplomacy, Bruce simply could not understand why his expedition did not merit the same generous treatment as those of Scott and Shackleton.

He was also aware that foreign Governments had allowed special grants for the publication of scientific reports. The German expedition received £27,000, Belgian £10,000, Swedish £5000, whilst the French Government covered the entire cost of publishing the results of Charcot's two expeditions.

When news of Captain Scott's death and the Terra Nova Expedition's disastrous outcome reached Britain in February 1913, Bruce expressed his genuine belief that the explorer's achievement was 'one of the greatest in the annals of exploration, for the British party had far greater difficulties in transit and route than the Norwegians', adding that 'Scott's death fighting against terrible odds was absolutely characteristic of the man'. Rudmose Brown, on the other hand, viewed the tragedy less generously:'Personally I feel the whole business is a colossal blunder, etc. [But can't well say this]', and continued, 'Bruce felt strongly the need of initiative to break orders on the part of his staff if they thought it essential'.

With Clements Markham still an enormously influential figure in the corridors of power in Whitehall, it was not surprising that Bruce's persistent lobbying for Government support yielded little result. As Markham wrote of the Discovery Expedition, 'The real objects are geographical discovery, and the opportunities for young naval officers to win distinction in time of peace'. Priority, prestige and patriotism were obviously still at stake, but the hidden agenda for polar expeditions was an imperialist–colonialist assumption of claiming new lands for the Crown, and that meant funding British endeavour, not Scottish.

In June 1912, whilst *Terra Nova* was still south, but before news of the death of Captain Scott and his companions reached Britain, Markham, now 82, contributed an article to the *Geographical Journal* entitled 'A Review of the Results of Antarctic Work originated by the Royal Geographical Society'. In reality it was a piece of self-praise and gave very little credit to any of the other expeditions of the Heroic Age. It served to infuriate Bruce and Rudmose Brown and their polar colleagues. Rudmose Brown wrote to Bruce (7 June):

> *That old fool and humbug Sir Clements Markham has an article in the June* Geographical Journal *on Twenty Years of Antarctic work. The article is mainly deigned to advertise himself and his beloved Captain Scott and to disparage every one else especially Amundsen and Shackleton.*
>
> *It is preposterous bunkum of that bloated old wind-bag to be allowed to pass unchallenged.*

Bruce replied on 10 June, sending a copy of a protest letter he had written to the current president of the Royal Geographical Society, Lord Curzon, and Rudmose Brown replied at once:

> *Your letter to Lord Curzon is brief. It might have been as well to remind him how important was the discovery of Coats Land and to what extent it changed the map of Antarctica.*
>
> *He advocated beating up a protest from all the expedition leaders of the first decade of the century and urged, 'Why not send a copy of the* GJ *[Geographical Journal] to these people (including Nansen on behalf of Amundsen) with a short note?*
>
> *It cannot possibly bring any change of advertisement against you, for that old fool's statements are unjust and untrue to all expeditions.*

Once the awful news of the deaths of Scott's polar party was confirmed in 1913, Bruce wrote immediately to Lady Scott, sending his sincere sympathy. There had never been any significant rivalry between Bruce and Scott; rather genuine admiration for each other's work.

Ernest Shackleton, however, received far less Government support for his second Antarctic expedition than Captain Scott. Undaunted, Shackleton wrote a confidential letter to Bruce on 20 August 1913, informing him of his progress thus far in raising funds from private sources:

... In strictest confidence I am sending you the programme of my proposed Trans-Antarctic Expedition. I am sending this particularly for the following reason. There is a dim hope that I may induce a very wealthy man I know to assist the Expedition, and I feel that before approaching him it would be well for me to have the opinions of one or two men eminent in this line or work and who can with authority state the value of such an Expedition.

Now it is well recognised that you are the one authority on the Weddell Sea side of the Antarctic, also that your knowledge of oceanographical and general scientific work is first class ....

I cannot look, nor am I going to try, for assistance from the Royal Geographical Society. You know as well as I do that they are hide-bound and narrow, and that neither you nor I happen to be particular pets of theirs.

I do not mind how much you enlarge on the value such an Expedition would be to science; also if you feel you can truthfully say that you think I am a suitable person to lead such an Expedition across the Continent.

Bruce lent his support, in spite of his anguish of knowing Shackleton's plans were almost identical to his own. To add to his woes, the 'very wealthy man' was probably the Scottish Dundee jute magnate Sir James Caird who sent Shackleton a cheque for £24,000. With £10,000 from Dudley Docker of BSA Birmingham, and a substantial amount from wealthy spinster Janet Stancomb-Wills, the ill-fated Endurance Expedition was able to go south.

News arrived in London that Shackleton, aboard *Endurance*, had reached the Weddell Sea by January 1915, but when the ship was frozen fast in the ice and eventually sunk nothing more was heard of their fate. Bruce was cautious but hopeful about *Endurance*. He wrote to Rudmose Brown on 14 April 1916 indicating that he had been in correspondence with Lady Shackleton, offering his services to the Shackleton relief committee and suggesting that *Endurance* might well turn up in Cape Town 'as late as May, or even in Australia'. He suggested that *Aurora* (at that time in New Zealand) should be repaired and refitted and made ready to land a party on Ross Island 'in case their services are required to unfold the present mystery there. I do not quite like the look of things as a whole, but I do not like to commit myself without knowing if I have all the available data, which so far I have only gleaned from the published telegrams.'

The men of *Endurance* were rescued after an epic voyage by Shackleton in the open boat *James Caird* to South Georgia. Help was raised there to save the *Endurance* crew.

Bruce's assistance had not been called upon, and he felt considerably aggrieved not to have been actively consulted by the Shackleton relief committee and the Royal Geographical Society. He wrote bitterly to Rudmose Brown on 6 May 1916:

There must be something hereditary surely in Presidents of the R.G.S., the way they systematically ignore the work of the 'Scotia' and the existence of many people who took part in the expedition. They pass over you actually working in their house; they avoid Mossman within half an hour's distance; and myself, I suppose, because of being north of the Tweed, they think dead.

It would have been difficult for Bruce not to imagine how his own expedition might have turned out. In his proposals for a second Scottish Antarctic expedition Bruce had not restricted the scientific work to oceanography, but planned terrestrial studies as well and a route that would take his party right across the Antarctic continent from the Weddell to the Ross Sea. This was a difficult journey that would only be completed fifty or so years later when Sir Vivian Fuchs and Sir Edmund Hillary successfully attempted the route in 1956-58 with the Commonwealth Trans-Antarctic Expedition. What the younger Bruce had sarcastically categorised as the 'boyish hunt for the Pole' was finally achieved with a thoroughly scientific expedition of which he would have approved. Fuchs, in recognition of the earlier aspirations of Bruce, took with him the flag of the Scottish National Antarctic Expedition that Bruce himself had intended to carry, and flew it at the South Pole.

The Polar Medal

The failure of successive Governments to award the Polar Medal to any of the members of the Scottish National Antarctic Expedition rankled with Bruce for the rest of his life. He declared his views with some vehemence in an issue (1908) of the *Scotia*, the Scottish nationalist publication:

In recent years there have been many signs of the strengthening of national spirit in Scotland. Not the least of these was Scotland taking her stand alongside the other nations of the world in the exploration of the Antarctic Regions by sending out the Scotia, 1902-1904, *well equipped with all the resources of modern science, and sailing under the name and title of the 'Scottish National Antarctic Expedition'.*

The time is therefore appropriate to call attention to the work of the Scotia, *and to see that researches carried out by a body of Scots which are internationally acknowledged to be at least equal to similar work carried out by Belgians, Swedes, French, and English, are not lost or allowed to lie fallow.*

Most strenuous efforts were made to secure for the Scotia *similar support to that which the English expedition received. The Admiralty, the Chancellor of the*

Exchequer, the Prime Minister, and others were approached, and even a moderate assistance was refused to the 'purely Scottish' Expedition.

On the return of the Scotia *the scientific staff, officers, and men received no official recognition or reward as did those of the* Discovery *and the two relief ships of the English expedition, although they had been doing exactly similar work. Assistance in the working up of the scientific material has also been refused from Government departments, unless the material gathered by the Scottish money was deposited in London, a condition that was not accepted.*

No more loyal part of the British Empire is to be found than Scotland ....

The original Arctic Medal was first issued in 1857 and awarded retrospectively to members of Arctic expeditions engaged in the search for both the North West and North East Passages. The Royal Naval ship *Isabella*, captained by Sir John Ross and assisted by Lieutenant Edward Parry in 1818, was the first to be so honoured, the award going generally to all ranks. Similarly most of the senior officers of the ships searching for the missing explorer Sir John Franklin between 1845 and 1848 were honoured with the medal.

The award was supplemented in 1904 by the introduction of the Polar Medal in recognition of the achievements of the Discovery Expedition, Scott's first expedition to the Antarctic, and awarded again to members of Shackleton's Nimrod Expedition of 1907-09. It has subsequently been awarded to many other British Antarctic expeditions and personnel on tours of duty in Antarctica, and from the 1930s to Arctic expeditions as well.

Recommendation for the award would be given to the Sovereign principally from the Council of the Royal Geographical Society.

Bruce, who had been awarded the Gold Medal of the Royal Scottish Geographical Society in 1904, expected London-based recognition for his officers and scientific staff. As the years passed he became increasingly exasperated and suspected that Markham, yet again, was behind the lack of interest.

Bruce decided to create his own award for the members of the Scotia Expedition and in 1906 commissioned a silver medal.

The obverse shows a terrestrial globe floating in space swathed in clouds, so orientated to display the Southern Ocean and neighbouring continents. Below it *Scotia* is beset in heavy ice off Coats Land in 71°S, with a flat-topped iceberg in the background. Encircling this is the legend, 'Scottish National Antarctic Expedition' with a figure of Saint Andrew and the Cross. The reverse side illustrates Omond House at the head of Scotia Bay and encircling this is a wreath of thistles supported by two flags – one the Scottish Lion, the other the flag of Saint Andrew with the letters

The Silver Medal created by Bruce. (*SPRI*)

'SNAE'. Above it is a scroll bearing the inscription 'for valuable services' and the recipient's name. Those who received the medal were the scientific staff (Rudmose Brown, Mossman, Harvey Pirie and Wilton); the ship's company (Captain Robertson, Davidson, Fitchie, MacDougall, Ramsay [posthumously], Gravill, Florence, William Smith, Murray, Anderson, Kerr, Martin, John Smith, Walker, Duncan and Low); and the home staff (Ferrier, Whitson and Nan Anderson [secretary]).

Ironically, however, the silver medal award served to further set apart the Scottish from the other British Antarctic expeditions, and Bruce's friends and colleagues continued to press for national recognition. It is interesting to note that similar treatment had been meted out to the illustrious Challenger Expedition (1872-76), which was primarily Scottish in personnel. John Murray proposed that a silver medal be struck, but HM Treasury refused to pay for it, and so Murray commissioned a medal and paid for it himself, sending replicas to those who had served in the expedition and to those who had written scientific reports. In 1898, however, Murray was awarded the rank of Knight Commander of the Order of the Bath by Queen Victoria.

There were some within the council of the Royal Geographical Society who were not unsympathetic to Bruce's cause, as this letter from the secretary Dr John Scott Keltie to council member Colonel H W Feilden CB indicates (28 January 1910):

My dear Feilden,

Bruce has evidently been at you as he has been at a great many other people and trying all the papers in order to attract attention to his troubles. If he had been a man of more tact than he seems to possess he would have fared better probably. I may tell you confidentially, as a member of the Council, that he would have been proposed for a Medal last year – in fact, he was proposed for a Medal last year, but he so irritated everybody by the way he behaved with reference to his expenses for a paper which he gave to us, that his name was withdrawn.

However, if you thought he really deserves a Medal, why not propose him for one of this year's Medals? That incident I refer to, is over and forgotten, and his claims might very well be brought up. I send you the statement which was drawn up before by Mill; that you might make use of with any additional points that you think might be brought forward on his behalf.

Rudmose Brown was no less angry than Bruce about the treatment of the Scottish National Antarctic Expedition by the British Government and wrote in 1913 to Lord Stair, at that time President of the Royal Scottish Geographical Society, urging further representation in London:

Soon after the return of the British Antarctic Expedition in Discovery *in 1904 the Polar Medal was initiated and awarded to all members of the expedition. It was also given to those who served on the two relief ships of the expedition, the* Morning *and the* Terra Nova. *The Scottish National Antarctic Expedition of Dr. W. S. Bruce which returned in 1904 received no award of the medal although it was subsequently bestowed on the members of Sir E.H. Shackleton's expedition in the* Nimrod. *This neglect of the Scottish Expedition is a slight to Scotland and to Scottish endeavour and it is as a medallist of the R.S.G.S. and a member of Dr. Bruce's* Scotia *expedition that I write to ask whether in your Lordship's opinion it is not a matter that the R.S.G.S. might not take up.*

The Discovery *was not a naval ship but sailed under the blue ensign. The* Nimrod *the same. The* Scotia *also flew the blue ensign. These expeditions were thus all on the same footing. That the medal was not struck exclusively for the* Discovery *is proved by its award to the officers and men of the* Nimrod.

The neglect of Government to grant the award to the officers and men of the Scotia *signifies but scant appreciation of the work of that expedition and is unfair to those who have earned it.*

If the R.S.G.S. were able to cause the oversight to be rectified they would show again the interest in Scottish exploration that they have already done so much to foster.

Lord Stair sent a brief reply pledging his support: 'I beg to acknowledge your letter of the 7th inst., which I will send on to May. Hope with a request that he will make enquiries in Parliament regarding the abominable treatment Dr Bruce has received.'

Bruce returned to the subject once more during World War I, perhaps not the best time to lobby any Member of Parliament. He had learned that

Douglas Mawson, leader of the Australasian Expedition (1911–14) and other members had been made recipients of the Polar Medal, and Bruce wrote to Dr John Horne, President of the Royal Society in Edinburgh, and received the following, dated 6 March 1915:

> *I duly received your letters about the Polar Medals awarded to the Mawson Expedition. Personally I agree with Rudmose Brown in thinking that an act of injustice has been done to the officers of the* Scotia. *Probably you are right in thinking that Markham is the cause. If so, he has much to answer for. I will consult some of the members of Council and see what can be done ....*

Rudmose Brown again threw his weight behind the argument and also wrote to Dr Horne reiterating the injustices:

> *Dr Bruce tells me that he has written to you to ask about the Polar Medal which was earned by the* Scotia *but withheld from us for reasons which were not convincing but which I believe he has told you. The Royal Scottish Geographical Society are trying to move the Government in the matter but I fear nothing will result unless Scottish opinion forcibly insists on this injustice being righted. Lately the medal has been granted to the Australian Antarctic Expedition and they certainly deserve it, but it seems not a little anomalous that a colonial expedition should receive it before a home one. It makes the unfairness of the Government even more glaring. At a time like this when most of the eligible members of the* Scotia *expedition are serving in His Majesty's Forces or otherwise helping the cause of Britain, the Government might surely reconsider their policies and not continue to cast this light on the work of Scotland in Antarctic exploration. For to single out Bruce's expedition as the only British expedition as unworthy of recognition is to cast an invidious slight on Bruce's work and one in which I need hardly say competent judges do not concur.*

In the summer of 1917 Bruce returned to the subject of the medal issue once again and wrote comprehensively to Charles Price on 24 August 1917. It appeared to have been the last salvo fired from Scotland on the subject. Clements Markham, the object of so much of Bruce's frustration, had died at the end of 1916.

> *Dear Mr. Price,*
>
> *In further reference to your two private letters of August 21st which I must again cordially thank you for, I have now looked out past correspondence back to 1900 on the subject. I have understood that it was King Edward that blocked the way and this was almost certainly after advice from the President of the Royal Geographical*

Society, viz. the late Sir Clements Markham, who was maliciously (as I can show from three of his letters in 1900) opposed to the Scottish Expedition from its inception, perhaps altogether not unassociated with personal enmity towards Sir John Murray, then President of the R.S.G.S. who officially made the first public announcement of the expedition, and with whom as a former pupil and assistant, I had specially confided instead of with Sir Clements Markham. Sir John saw these letters, and advised me in, and approved of, my answers to them.

Markham caused official estrangement between me and the Royal Geographical Society, on account of his disparagement of 'Scotia' work, which was not cleared up until I received a most cordial letter from his successor in the Presidency, viz. Sir George D. Taubman-Goldie, P.C. etc. in 1907, asking me to lecture to the Society and adding, 'I need hardly tell you that our Society has always followed with interest your excellent work for the last 20 years'.

I thanked Sir George Taubman-Goldie, agreed to lecture, and told him that I could not help comparing his attitude with that of his predecessor who had called my work 'mischievous rivalry'.

In 1910 the Society (Major Leonard Darwin President) conferred on me the Patrons Gold Medal with the approval of King Edward for my work.

Colonel H.W. Feilden, C.B., of Arctic fame, a Councillor, was largely responsible for this medal being conferred on me, and has told me that Markham, as a Councillor and past President, strongly opposed it.

In November 1913 (Lord Curzon President) I was elected Life Member of R.G.S. without payment, as one of those 'distinguished for their services to Geographical Science'.

I only mention these personal matters to suggest that as leader of the S.N.A.E. the expedition probably took a part in Antarctic exploration at least equal to any other British expedition, upon the members of which the Polar Medal has been conferred by the King.

Sir John Murray, Mr. J.Y. Buchanan, F.R.S. and others, resigned from the Joint Antarctic Committee of Royal Society and Royal Geographical Society because Markham's attitude was opposed to their views, and Markham mainly carried things through for the 1st English Antarctic Expedition, which Murray, Buchanan and others thought better than a public fight and fiasco in which they had no intention to share join responsibility. Scott was Markham's protégé, and Markham thought it necessary, in order to uphold Scott, that I should be obliterated, just as he did long before in the case of Dr. John Rae and Sir Leopold McClintock, which Dr. Rae's widow could still tell you about. Markham did the same to others whom he considered 'mischievous rivals'. Always a policy of stealthy obliteration.

Doubtlessly as a long standing and powerful President of the R.G.S. King Edward listened to Markham regarding the comparative merits of the 'Discovery' and 'Scotia' expeditions, and acted accordingly, but, personally, I cannot see why

King George should confirm an error of judgement, if it be such, of his Father, but would surely rather seek to rectify it.

I write strongly about this, because it is more for others than myself. I would not move a foot for a medal or other award that was not freely given, but what about my Colleagues! What about the slur on the 'Scotia's' work! The slur on British Oceanography and exploration! And the slight to Scotia men meeting men, who have actually in some cases done far less in Antarctic work and hardship and who yet wear the white ribbon?

No man in the world is a more experienced or successful ice navigator than Captain Robertson, and if he had been well and in charge of Shackleton's ship, it would not have been lost in the Weddell Sea any more than the 'Scotia'. Yet Robertson is dying without his well won white ribbon! The Mate is dead! The Second Mate is dead!! The Chief Engineer is dead!!! Everyone as good men as have ever served on any Polar Expedition, yet they did not receive the white ribbon.

Surely it can merely be treated as an omission by the King, the public need never know that King Edward even considered the matter.

I have no idea who the best person is to explain the position to the King. I think he would do the right thing if he knew Markham had advised his father contrary to official R.G.S. opinion.

Markham probably believed that I had detracted money from the Scott expedition, but this was not so. The late James Coats, who gave nearly £24,000 out of the £35,000 raised by me and Major Andrew Coats, who gave £7,000, quite clearly would not have given this money to an expedition outside Scotland. James Coats actually bought out an American Subscriber to make it purely Scottish. I had served under Major Andrew Coats, and both were personal friends, since 1898.

Scott and I were always good friends, in spite of Markham.

Regarding the Admiralty, I will sit tight till you are able to see me in October. With kind regards, and many thanks for great kindness ....

St Abbs, Seychelles

Support for Bruce from London remained negligible. He even encountered great difficulty obtaining a post with the Admiralty during the early part of the war, despite repeatedly offering his services. Surely his specialist knowledge and experience of the oceanography of high-latitude waters would have guaranteed him a place in the decision-making process. Bruce once again blamed the indifference of the Admiralty on his nationalistic views, but needing some form of employment he accepted an offer from his long-standing friend Burn Murdoch to become a director and manager of a Scottish-Norwegian whaling company called St Abbs, working from a base in the Seychelles.

The company operated from the island of St Anne, four miles offshore from the capital Mahé, and was registered with a secretary, A Thomson, with offices at 140 Princes Street, Edinburgh. It was formed in 1913 with directors William Gordon Burn Murdoch, Charles Urmston and Patrick Currie of Scotland, Alexander Heyder of Liverpool, and two Norwegian merchants of Tønsberg. They owned two whalers, the diesel motor vessel *St Ebba* and the steam whaler *Mossel*, and hired a second steam whaler, *Rusheen*. The whaling grounds were some 60-80 miles (97-129km) east of Seychelles, and between October 1914 and July 1915, 122 sperm whales were killed, producing 2191 barrels of oil shipped primarily to Britain.

Bruce left Scotland to manage the company's whaling station in April 1915 and wrote to Rudmose Brown on 4 February 1915:

> *I shall be closely tied to the business affairs of the Company and shall have little opportunity for carrying on any scientific investigations. Still I want to keep my eyes open and would like to have all the scientific literature I can on the Seychelles.*

Bruce was well received in Mahé. There was great expectation of his abilities, as this report by the Governor, Sir Charles O'Brien, to the Secretary of State for the Colonies states (17 February):

> *When Dr. Bruce of oceanographical fame was sent out in April of last year I hoped the affairs of the Company would be put on a firm basis and the losses due to reckless expenditure written off.*

But Bruce was still a man of science rather than a man of business and although he did everything possible to turn the company around, the war made the raising of further capital impossible. When the *St Ebba* was wrecked off the coast of South Africa, the firm was forced into liquidation in August 1915. Bruce returned to Scotland and in the following year finally gained a relatively minor post in the Admiralty, working on manuals for navigation.

References

Bruce, William Speirs: *Polar Exploration* (London, 1911).
Poulson, N: *The White Ribbon* (London, 1968).
Rudmose Brown, Robert Neal: *A Naturalist at the Poles* (London, 1923).

CHAPTER 11

THE LAST YEARS

BY 1919 the achievements of the Scottish National Antarctic Expedition had largely been forgotten. Bruce's health was beginning to fail and he was admitted to the Royal Infirmary Hospital in Edinburgh for an operation. His last visit to Spitsbergen in 1920 was in a non-executive capacity as guest of the Syndicate.

As he was estranged from his wife Jessie, only Rudmose Brown and a few of Bruce's academic and business associates were around to witness his final days. To the end they worried about his health and reputation as this letter written in October 1920 from Alfred Aitken to Arthur Hinks, secretary of the Royal Geographical Society, illustrates:

> … I had an opportunity yesterday of communicating to Dr Bruce your letter to me of the 7th. He was greatly pleased to hear about the coming presentation of the Livingstone medal on 20th. He quite broke down when he heard that the subject of the Meeting would be the 'Future of Polar Research', and I think he realised the very slight prospect he has of taking part in any such work. I mentioned your suggestion that Mr Wordie might receive the medal on his behalf and he appreciated your thoughtfulness. This morning I have a letter from Mr Wordie to say that he will be very pleased to do so.
>
> I do hope there will be some reference at the Meeting to Dr Bruce's work in connection with Polar Research. In his present condition there could be no better medicine for him! I am glad to say that on the whole he is making good progress towards recovery, but his locomotion is not improving and any attempt to do a little more today than he did yesterday seems to set him back. He is still in the Royal Infirmary under the special care of Professor Meakins who thinks that there is steady, though slow, improvement.

In the event the medal was received by Rudmose Brown in the presence of Bruce's father and sisters.

Bruce left the Royal Infirmary for a short time, but was admitted to Liberton Hospital the following year. He died there on 28 October 1921.

The funeral of William Speirs Bruce was held on 2 November, the

anniversary of the 1902 departure of *Scotia* for Antarctica. In accordance
with his instructions, his body was cremated in Glasgow and his ashes
conveyed to the Southern Ocean. In his will he requested that the ashes
should be scattered at sea in longitude 10° to 15°E in a high latitude.
Accordingly the magistrate of South Georgia, Edward B Binnie, on Easter
Monday 1923, together with the manager of the Grytviken Whaling
Station and some of his officers, sailed from the harbour on the whale-
catcher *Symra* and scattered Bruce's ashes on the sea after a brief ceremony.

A commemorative ceremony and the casting of a wreath in the Scotia Sea
took place in 1988, jointly by Robert Headland, archivist of the Scott
Polar Research Institute, and Hans Kjell Larsen of Norway, grandson of Carl
Anton Larsen, founder of the first shore-based whaling station on South
Georgia in 1904. In March 1997 the author of this volume cast a small bunch
of flowers to the sea off the harbour in Grytviken in memory of Bruce after
addressing a gathering of members of the National Trust for Scotland and
explaining the importance of the work of Bruce during the Heroic Age of
Polar Exploration.

In Scotland his name is all but forgotten and no plaque or statue has ever
been raised to his memory. His ideals of a Scottish oceanographical institute
came to naught, his Scottish Spitsbergen Syndicate did not mine any
commercial minerals, not one of the Scotia Expedition members received the
Polar Medal, and credit for the conception of the Edinburgh Zoological

The author pays tribute to Bruce at Grytviken, South Georgia.

Gardens was largely bestowed on others. Yet his selfless devotion to polar science was worthy of remembrance, and his unassuming manner combined with dogged determination to ensure that Scotland's place in the history of polar exploration would be forever recognised, deserve better than the fading memories of a few scholars. Rudmose Brown wrote to Samuel Bruce after his son's funeral:

> *As a companion of your son's on many of his expeditions and his friend for nearly twenty years, may I express to you my sympathy with you and your daughters and Sheila on the great loss you have sustained? To me your son was the truest friend I have ever had. Without his devotion and his thoughtfulness on many occasions in Arctic and Antarctic I could never have come through some experiences. And what I feel for him as a leader and comrade is shared by others who accompanied his expeditions. He never spared himself to help his comrades and never expected as much of them as of himself. It is sad to think that he has gone at so early an age but at least it is a comfort to know that his work will always endure. And that is the most that he would ask for. His name is imperishably enrolled among the world's great explorers and the martyrs to unselfish scientific devotion.*

Although the Heroic Age of Polar Exploration concluded decades ago, there is still a scientific imperative for research in these far away and exotic regions. William Speirs Bruce would have appreciated the designation of Antarctica as a 'Continent and Ocean for Science'. Rudmose Brown, however, in his *Scotia* diary, perhaps captured the spirit of Antarctica for them all:

> *It is very beautiful to look on this panorama of sea and snow-capped mountains, when the sun is glistening all the peaks and ridges – or even when the wind and driving snow is tearing over them, they look very grand, half shrouded in the mist. Of course there are prettier places and more sympathetic places, but I doubt if any more absolutely beautiful.*

References

Anon: 'Obituary of W S Bruce' in *Dispatch* (Edinburgh, 31 October 1921).
Anon: 'Obituary of W S Bruce' in *Glasgow Herald* (Glasgow, 31 October 1921).
Anon: 'Obituary of W S Bruce' in *Scotsman* (Edinburgh, 31 October 1921).
Burn Murdoch, William Gordon: *Modern Whaling and Bear Hunting* (London, 1917).
Markham, Clements Robert: 'Review of the Results of Twenty Years of Antarctic Work', originated by the Royal Geographical Society in *Geographical Journal* (London, June 1912), vol XXXIX.
Ritchie, J: 'Obituary of W S Bruce' in *Scottish Naturalist* (Edinburgh, 1921), vol 119/120.
Rudmose Brown, Robert Neal: 'Obituary of W S Bruce' in *Scottish Geographical Magazine* (Edinburgh, 1922), vol 37.

APPENDIX I

SELECTED WORKS
BY WILLIAM SPEIRS BRUCE

Report on the Scientific Results of the Voyage of SY Scotia during the years 1902, 1903, and 1904, under the leadership of William S Bruce, LLD, FRSE:

Volume I – (published in 1992)	Volume V – *Zoology, Invertebrates*
Volume II – *Physics*	Volume VI – *Zoology, Invertebrates*
Volume III – *Botany*	Volume VII – *Zoology, Invertebrates*
Volume IV – *Zoology*	

[Apart from volume I, published in 1992, the reports were published between 1907 and 1920 (Edinburgh: Scottish Oceanographical Laboratory)]

Polar Exploration (London: Home University Library, 1911).
The Log of the Scotia *Expedition, 1902-04* (edited by Peter Speak) (Edinburgh: Edinburgh University Press, 1992).

William Speirs Bruce also published many academic papers in *Scottish Geographical Magazine, Geographical Journal*, and *Transactions of the Royal Society of Edinburgh*, as well as several more popular articles.

APPENDIX II

CHRONOLOGY OF VOYAGES

1892-93	Dundee Whaling Expedition, *Balaena*, to Antarctica
1896-97	Jackson-Harmsworth Expedition, *Windward*, to Franz Josef Land
1898	Coats Expedition, *Blencathra*, to Novaya Zemlya
1898	Prince of Monaco Expedition, *Princesse Alice*, to Spitsbergen
1899	Prince of Monaco Expedition, *Princesse Alice*, to Spitsbergen
1902-04	Scottish National Antarctic Expedition, *Scotia*
1906	Bruce Topographical Survey, *Princesse Alice*, to Prince Charles Foreland, Spitsbergen
1907	Bruce Expedition, *Fønix*, conclude Topographical Survey of Prince Charles Foreland
1909	Prospecting for Scottish Spitsbergen Syndicate, *Conqueror*, in Spitsbergen
1912	Prospecting for Scottish Spitsbergen Syndicate, postal vessel *Dion*, and return in *William Munroe* in West Spitsbergen
1914	Prospecting for Scottish Spitsbergen Syndicate, *Pelikane*, in Spitsbergen
1915-16	Whaling Manager for St Abbs Whaling Company, Seychelles; owned whalers *St Ebba* (diesel) and *Mossel* (steam); hired steam whaler *Rusheen*
1919	Prospecting for Scottish Spitsbergen Syndicate, *Petunia*, in Spitsbergen
1920	Prospecting for Scottish Spitsbergen Syndicate, *Easonian*, in Spitsbergen

APPENDIX III

AWARDS AND PRIZES

1904	Gold Medal of the Royal Scottish Geographical Society
1906	Honorary degree of LLD from the University of Aberdeen
1910	Patron's Medal of the Royal Geographical Society
1913	Neill prize and Medal of the Royal Society of Edinburgh
1920	Livingstone Medal of the American Geographical Society

THE BRUCE MEMORIAL PRIZE

The Bruce Memorial Prize was instituted in his honour in 1923 by a joint committee of the Royal Society of Edinburgh, the Royal Physical Society, and the Royal Scottish Geographical Society, to award young scientists carrying out research in high latitudes. There is no special residential qualification and the award for notable research in the fields of zoology, geology, meteorology, oceanography and geography, made every two years initially, can be made to scientists from any part of the world. So far, those honoured in this way are the following polar explorers and scientists:

1926	James Mann Wordie	1954	Richard M Laws
1928	H U Sverdrup	1956	J W Cowie
1930	N A Mackintosh	1958	Hal Lister
1932	Henry Gino Watkins	1960	J MacDowell
1936	James W S Marr	1962	Ken V Blaiklock
1938	Alexander Glen	1964	Martin W Holdgate
1940	Brian Roberts	1966	Stan Evans
1942	G C L Bertram	1968	W S B Paterson
1944	Tom H Manning	1972	Peter Friend
1946	Pat D Baird	1977	Peter Wadhams
1948	W A Deer	1980	Andrew Clarke
1950	M J Dunbar	1987	J E Gordon
1952	Gordon de Q Robin	1994	Ian Boyd
		1999	David R Marchant

GENERAL INDEX

INDEX OF SHIPS